The Policy-Making Process

PRENTICE HALL FOUNDATIONS OF MODERN POLITICAL SCIENCE SERIES

Robert A. Dahl, Editor

THE AGE OF IDEOLOGY—POLITICAL THOUGHT, 1750 TO THE PRESENT, Second Edition
   by Isaac Kramnick and Frederick M. Watkins

THE ANALYSIS OF INTERNATIONAL RELATIONS, Third Edition
   by Karl W. Deutsch

CONGRESS AND THE PRESIDENCY, Fourth Edition
   by Nelson W. Polsby

DATA ANALYSIS FOR POLITICS AND POLICY
   by Edward R. Tufte

MODERN POLITICAL ANALYSIS, Fifth Edition
   by Robert A. Dahl

MODERN POLITICAL ECONOMY
   by Norman Frohlich and Joe A. Oppenheimer

THE POLICY-MAKING PROCESS, Third Edition
   by Charles E. Lindblom and Edward J. Woodhouse

Charles E. Lindblom
Yale University

Edward J. Woodhouse
Rensselaer Polytechnic Institute

The Policy-Making Process

THIRD EDITION

PRENTICE HALL, UPPER SADDLE RIVER, NEW JERSEY 07458

Library of Congress Cataloging-in-Publication Data

Lindblom, Charles Edward, (date)
    The policy-making process / Charles E. Lindblom, Edward J. Woodhouse.
—3rd ed.
        p.   cm. — (Prentice Hall foundations of modern political
science series)
    Includes bibliographical references and indexes.
    ISBN 0-13-682360-2
    1. United States—Politics and government.   2. Policy sciences.
3. Power (Social sciences)   I. Woodhouse, Edward J.   II. Title.
III. Series.
JK271.L52   1993
320'.6—dc20   92-28729
                                                                    CIP

Acquisitions editor: Julie Berrisford
Editorial assistant: Nicole Signoretti
Editorial/production supervision and
    interior design: Mary McDonald
Copy editor: Patricia Daly
Cover design: Karen Marsilio
Prepress buyer: Kelly Behr
Manufacturing buyer: Mary Ann Gloriande

Printed in the United States of America
11

ISBN 0-13-682360-2

PRENTICE-HALL INTERNATIONAL (UK) LIMITED, *London*
PRENTICE-HALL OF AUSTRALIA PTY. LIMITED, *Sydney*
PRENTICE-HALL CANADA INC., *Toronto*
PRENTICE-HALL HISPANOAMERICANA, S.A., *Mexico*
PRENTICE-HALL OF INDIA PRIVATE LIMITED, *New Delhi*
PRENTICE-HALL OF JAPAN, INC., *Tokyo*
PEARSON EDUCATION ASIA PTE. LTD., *Singapore*
EDITORA PRENTICE-HALL DO BRASIL, LTDA., *Rio de Janeiro*

Contents

Preface   vii

Acknowledgments   ix

PART I   INTRODUCTION   1

Chapter 1   The Challenges Facing Policy Making   2

Chapter 2   The Limits of Analysis   13

Chapter 3   The Potential Intelligence of Democracy   23

**PART II   CONVENTIONAL GOVERNMENT
AND POLITICS   33**

Chapter 4   The Imprecision of Voting   34

Chapter 5   Elected Functionaries   45

Chapter 6   Bureaucratic Policy Making   57

Chapter 7   Interest Groups in Policy Making   73

✸ **PART III   BROADER INFLUENCES
ON POLICY MAKING   89**

Chapter 8   The Position of Business in Policy Making   90

Chapter 9   Political Inequality   104

Chapter 10   Impaired Inquiry   114

PART IV   IMPROVING POLICY MAKING   125

Chapter 11   Making the Most of Analysis   126

Chapter 12   More Democracy?   139

Name Index   151

Subject Index   156

Preface

Each edition of *The Policy-Making Process* has sought to provide political science scholars and students with resources not available in standard texts. The book's central theme is that there are sharp constraints on what can be achieved through policy analysis and other "rational" methods for understanding social problems; this is largely because uncertainty and disagreement are fundamental facts of political life, facts that cannot be wished away by even the most rigorous analysis.

Political interactions and flawed human judgments play a primary role in making policy, and these necessarily involve partisan disagreements that are settled by voting or other manifestations of power. Hence, anyone who wants to understand what goes wrong in the effort to use government to promote human well-being needs to comprehend how power relations shape and mis-shape public policy—and to probe how power relations might be restructured to produce better policy.

The first edition of *The Policy-Making Process* in 1968 sought simply to help bring the subject of public policy onto the mainstream agenda of political science. That task had been largely achieved by 1980, when the second edition argued for taking greater account of the influential role of business in policy making. Part of that task, too, has now been achieved, with political economy incorporated into both policy studies and political science more generally. The second edition dealt also with the pernicious effects of political inequality, especially the possibility that policy ideas are systematically misshaped by the pro-business cultures of market-oriented democracies.

While those themes remain central in this substantially rewritten third edition, even more sustained attention is focused on the larger political setting within which public policy deliberations and manipulations occur. In particular, we attempt to discern the processes by which the competition of ideas is stunted in contemporary political systems. The ability of every contemporary democracy to probe social problems and policy options is systematically crippled, undermining both the extent of democracy and the degree of intelligence brought to bear in policy making. This third edition also ventures into the perilous task of prescribing how public policy can be improved, a change of tack due partly to the influence of the new coauthor, Woodhouse, and partly to the evolution of Lindblom's thinking about the appropriateness of informed and thoughtful partisanship in social science.

One set of prescriptions concerns how policy professionals can do a better job of catalyzing debate about social problems and policy options. Whereas most policy research focuses on informing political elites, we suggest that helping ordinary people to think more clearly about social problems and possibilities is the best hope for shaping a better world. To do this will require a certain kind of deliberately *partisan* rather than professedly noncommitted analysis. Improved analysis also will face up to the inevitability of uncertainty and disagreement and will offer sustained guidance regarding the tasks of coping with uncertainty and learning from experience at a reasonable cost.

A complementary set of prescriptions focuses on the need for rethinking and changing power relations to better promote the intelligence of democracy. The linchpin of such an endeavor would entail curbing the privileged position of business. Second is to promote a more vigorous competition of ideas, thereby reducing the extent of impaired thinking among ordinary people as well as among political elites. Third is to move toward more genuine political equality, so that each person's problems, aspirations, and ideas have a better chance of registering effectively in the policy-making process.

We thank the many fellow scholars and students who have offered suggestions for improving *The Policy-Making Process,* especially Frank Laird and Steven Shulman. We dedicate this edition to the students who will use it, in the hope that their generation will learn how to extend the intelligence of democracy.

Charles E. Lindblom
Edward J. Woodhouse

Acknowledgments

The aim of this series is to provide a group of books that will integrate the major aspects of modern political science. Guided by the highest standards of contemporary scholarship and a concern for the major historic problems of politics, the series will make available the fruits of the most recent empirical and theoretical studies.

Reviewers of *The Policy-Making Process* (third edition): Richard A. Loverd, Villanova University; Jerold L. Waltman, University of Southern Mississippi; Michael E. Kraft, University of Wisconsin at Green Bay.

PART I

INTRODUCTION

Chapter 1

The Challenges Facing Policy Making

Why are humans not more effective in actually solving social problems? Why do avowedly democratic governments so often appear unresponsive to many of their citizens?[1] In some of the most serious failures of political and economic policy making in the twentieth century, governments and businesses have

- Expended more than $5 trillion on military weaponry, accompanied by untold fear and nearly 100 million lives taken in violent conflict;
- Introduced into ecosystems approximately 100,000 synthetic organic chemicals, without much knowledge of their carcinogenic and other harmful properties;
- Allowed an estimated 20 million children and adults annually to die of malnutrition and related diseases;
- Depleted far more of the earth's irreplaceable oil and natural gas reserves than required for efficient transport, heating, and industry;
- Expended hundreds of billions of dollars on giant nuclear reactors that are neither economically nor politically acceptable in most nations;
- Initiated partial depletion of the ozone layer, and perhaps precipitated global climate warming; and
- Failed to mount adequately funded international birth control and economic assistance programs, with the result that world population will increase by some one billion persons in the 1990s.

[1]We refer to political systems with genuinely free elections as "democracies," though at various points questioning the extent to which they really are very democratic.

Added to these and other grand assaults are the myriad social problems so familiar to everyone: poverty, racism, gender bias, child abuse, alcohol and drug addiction, unhappy marriages, unsuccessful educational systems, highway deaths and mutilations, suburban sprawl, spiralling medical costs, political corruption, mindless television—the list seems endless.

These undeniable realities mock human aspirations for intelligent public policy. Indeed, if experience is a reliable guide, the odds of moving toward intelligent, democratic government are unpromising. It is not surprising, then, that many people retire to a private life of such enjoyment as they find possible within the constraints of a problem-ridden civilization.[2] On the other hand, those who continue to pursue the possibility that humanity's future might be guided by significantly wiser decisions than its past can point to hopeful signs such as growing environmental consciousness, the end of the Cold War, and reduced discrimination against women, ethnic minorities, and homosexuals in some nations.

Both the successes and failures raise questions. If humans are not forever doomed to live with relatively undemocratic and relatively unintelligent policy making, it makes sense to inquire systematically into what stands in the way. "What interferes with intelligence and with popular control in attacking social problems?" sounds like a straightforward question that ought to be easy to answer. It turns out to be a formidable task, requiring substantial rethinking of what social problem solving is all about.

POLICY MAKING BROADLY CONCEIVED

Who makes policy? Because presidents and prime ministers, cabinet secretaries and ministers, mayors and governors, legislators and bureaucrats are the most visible parts of the policy-making process, they tend to receive disproportionate attention in media coverage, in courses about politics and public policy, and in the public mind. Yet few people make the equivalent mistake about economic life. Goods and services obviously are produced through a complex economic *system,* with products emerging through the contributions of millions of people interacting with each other. Public policies likewise are made via a complex political system and cannot be understood primarily by looking at the actions of President Clinton, German Chancellor Kohl, or other top government officials.

In attempting to grasp and synthesize the complex set of forces that together produces effects called "policies," therefore, this book does not make governmental institutions and office holders the sole object of study. Elected

[2]On political avoidance, see Herbert J. Gans, *Middle American Individualism* (New York: The Free Press, 1988).

and appointed officials clearly are the ones who most directly enact and administer laws. But these proximate policy makers typically dispute over a relatively narrow range of alternatives, winnowed down to fit into a broad area of basic agreement.

> In a sense, what we ordinarily describe as democratic "politics" is merely the chaff. It is the surface manifestation, representing superficial conflicts. Prior to politics, beneath it, enveloping it, restricting it, conditioning it, is the underlying consensus on policy that usually exists in the society among a predominant portion of the politically active members.[3]

If social problem solving is faring poorly, if the policy-making process is yielding seriously defective outcomes, then it may be desirable to greatly expand the range of policy alternatives being considered. That will require looking at the deeper processes by which the "underlying consensus" is formed.

Such a task is not well served by conventional political terminology, which suggests that the impetus for policy comes primarily from a few "leaders"—and implies that everyone else is a "follower." To the contrary, politicians and bureaucrats often serve as lenses through which are refracted diverse pressures, ideas, questions, problems, and policy options, emanating directly and indirectly from countless sources. This is not to deny that government officials have their own agendas as well: They protect programs, build careers, increase their authority, promote certain visions of the public interest, and sometimes enrich their own coffers. These goals they pursue by adapting to and using the flow of problems and policy ideas, information and political opportunities flowing through their domains. But "lead"? Not primarily.

Because so many people and social forces influence policy outcomes, it is misleading to refer to those in positions of authority as "*the* policy makers" or "leaders" or "decision makers." Unfortunately, no entirely adequate replacement for these comfortable terms is available in English. This book uses the somewhat awkward and unfamiliar term *functionary,* meaning a person who performs a certain function, especially an official.[4] What the word lacks in elegance and familiarity, it perhaps makes up for by being more accurate. Since part of our aim is to help readers *unlearn* some of what usually is taught about political life, the very awkwardness of the term may serve as a reminder of how broad the policy-making process actually is, a reminder not to focus excessively on government officials.

In keeping with this emphasis, in addition to covering legislators, interest groups, and other governmental parts of the policy-making process, we pay

---

[3]Robert A. Dahl, *A Preface to Democratic Theory* (Chicago: University of Chicago Press, 1956), p. 132.
[4]In French, the term for government official is "fonctionnaire."

at least equal attention to broader influences on policy making. These include humans' limited capacities for inquiry into complex problems, the frequent conflict between reasoned judgment and the exercise of political power, the central role of business in policy making, and socioeconomic and political inequality. For reasons that will become apparent, understanding these broader aspects of policy making goes a long way toward unraveling the mystery of why governmental problem solving is not more effective—and suggests beginnings for how to do better.

COGNITIVE LIMITS AND IMPAIRMENTS

A basic discrepancy exists between humans' mental capacities and the complexities of policy problems. Even when extended by a range of devices from written language to electronic computers, the mind at its best simply cannot grasp the complexity of social reality. Recipient of a Nobel prize for his studies of cognitive decision processes, Herbert Simon argues that "The capacity of the human mind for formulating and solving complex problems is very small compared with the size of the problems whose solution is required for objectively rational behavior in the real world—or even for a reasonable approximation to such objective rationality."[5]

Take even an extremely simple policy problem: Should a city government introduce one-way traffic on a downtown street? Policy makers cannot know all the effects on traffic (including diversion of congestion to other streets), on convenience of citizens, or on the profitability of businesses in the area. Even the best analytic techniques, which may require expertise unavailable to the city, could answer these questions only with inconclusive estimates that might turn out to be misleading.

Traffic obviously is a much easier subject than most local problems, such as how to deal with overcrowded jails, drug addiction, or AIDS. It certainly is less complex than budget deficits and many other policy issues confronted in Washington, Paris, or Tokyo. And the difficulties of predicting traffic pale in comparison with trying to understand the effects of German reunification or foreseeing how to bring real peace to the Middle East.

There is a deep and persistent unwillingness in Western culture to acknowledge the difficulties arising from the world's complexity and humans' modest cognitive abilities. As a result, attempts to understand social problem solving often go awry from the start. For unless human limits are taken very seriously, it is impossible to appreciate the magnitude of the task facing the political system; and unless political action is adjusted to take account of the

---

[5]Herbert A. Simon, *Models of Man* (New York: John Wiley & Sons, 1957), p. 198.

fact that complex problems cannot be understood fully, policy making will fare much worse than it needs to.

Added to human biological limitations are socially caused impairments in people's capacities for thoughtful probing of social problems and policy options. From parents forcing toddlers to conform to arbitrary standards, to schools numbing so many young minds, to the lack of a real competition of ideas on most broadcast news and commentary programs, social institutions impede people from developing and exercising their capacity for reason.

If people are impaired as citizens in their capacities for appraising public issues, what are the effects on policy making? It is worth exploring whether the long-term hopes for human betterment may rest partly on improvements in people's capacity for thinking about their problems, together with improvements in elites' capacities and incentives for listening to ordinary people. Cognitive limits, socially induced impairments, and the reduction of impairment constitute one central theme of the book.

ANALYSIS VERSUS POWER

Does improved social problem solving require bringing far more information and systematic thought into the policy-making process? Many people believe so, and the study of policy making has paid special attention to the roles of information and analysis, with some books and courses focusing almost entirely on these intellectual components of political life. In the face of problems such as the greenhouse effect, the savings and loan debacle, and recurrent periods of high unemployment, demands for more informed policies seem eminently sensible.[6]

Thoughtful critics point out that intellectual approaches to problems sometimes become preoccupied with bloodless analytical categories and statistical treatments carried to indefensible extremes. Nevertheless, the demand for more information and analysis is unmistakable, a demand that seems to call for a reduction of partisan political conflict, of political maneuvering, of power, of "politics."

Yet the desire for popular influence over government requires that policy making remain political. Few would wish to go so far toward technocratic governance by experts as to surrender the right to a vote, and most people expect elected functionaries to consider ordinary citizens' opinions on various issues. Although people believe that governments need more research and analysis on policy problems, then, they apparently intend that their elected

---

[6]These high expectations for analysis often mix with some anxieties about who can be trusted to do the analyzing. Would one believe a public utility company's study of the need for more nuclear generation of electric power? Or the Defense Department's estimates of a new weapon's long-term costs?

officials somehow should call on the services of analysts and experts without abdicating political authority to them.

Thus, a deep conflict runs through common attitudes toward policy making. People want policy to be informed and well analyzed, perhaps even correct or scientific; yet they also want policy making to be democratic and hence necessarily an exercise of power. Of course, all governmental policy making can be considered political, since it involves the use of authority. By using the term *political* more narrowly, however, it becomes possible to contrast reasoned persuasion with power: reaching policy choices by informed analysis and thoughtful discussion, versus setting policy by bargaining, trading of favors, voting, or otherwise exerting power. In this sense, politics is prominent in congressional decisions on the location of military bases in the various states, while analysis is more central in decisions of the Federal Reserve Board on monetary policy. But analysis and politics always intertwine.

Many democratic theorists and social thinkers have tried to resolve the conflict. They argue that open political interchange in a democratic society—a "competition of ideas"—is the best road to truth, that democratic politics offers the best chance for informed and reasoned policy making. Even if it is the best road, however, it looks perilous. Many people distrust democratic politics because they perceive the competition of ideas to bring not reason but contentiousness into policy making. This suggests a serious conflict: To enhance the role of reason and analysis in policy making, must a society surrender some aspects of democracy? Or, despite intermittent conflict, can a society enjoy both more reasoned and more democratic policy making? The relation of knowledge and power is a second central theme for this entire book.

THE POLICY-MAKING ROLES OF BUSINESS

Important public tasks are delegated to the business sector in societies that employ market economies; since the demise of centrally planned economies in the USSR and eastern Europe, this includes all democratic systems and most of the rest of the world. Market-oriented societies can be said to have a second set of "public officials": business managers who organize the labor force, allocate resources, plan capital investments, and otherwise undertake many of the organizational tasks of economic life. Corporate executives, not government officials, set most policies regarding production of electric power, transportation services, entertainment, insurance, steel, housing, food, computers, newspapers, television, toys, and many other goods and services.[7]

Even though these functions are not governmental, they are public in the

[7]On delegation of much economic decision making to the business sector, see Charles E. Lindblom, *Politics and Markets: The World's Political-Economic Systems* (New York: Basic Books, 1977).

sense of mattering to everyone, and decisions about them are as important as decisions made by government. Creation of jobs and the resulting employment or unemployment, price levels, and overall expansion or contraction of the economy are influenced by government policies, of course; but they depend even more directly on the actions of business executives and other participants in the market system.

The significance of business decision making cannot be denied by claiming that business executives enjoy no discretion but are compelled to do what customers want. Consumers indeed exercise loose control over business decisions by "voting" with dollars when they buy or refuse to buy. But consumers' influence is limited, at best, to specifying roughly what goods and services succeed in winning an ongoing niche in retail stores. Consumers have little impact on whether workers are displaced by robots, or on where General Motors locates a new assembly plant for the Saturn automobile; consumers do not decide whether aerosol sprays will use dangerous chemical propellants, or on whether word processors are used to make secretarial jobs more interesting or more pressured.[8] If, through competition, consumers press to keep costs down, corporate executives nevertheless retain a great deal of discretion over what and how they produce, affect the environment, and use the workforce.

Business executives obviously make wise decisions as well as bad ones, just as governmental officials do; the quality of decisions varies. What remains invariant is that there is this second set of public officials, and that policy making by the "private sector" constitutes a system of control over society's directions that rivals government in overall import. This book analyzes governmental policy processes, not those pertaining to economic transactions in the market; but the two systems, each engaged in public policy making, intertwine frequently and with significant consequence.

This is true in part because, as everyone knows, along with the good it achieves, business life simultaneously produces many serious problems: abandoned toxic waste dumps and other environmental pollution, automobiles with safety defects that kill and maim, advertising that misleads; the list is long. Indeed, it is perhaps not unfair to say that business executives often have strong incentives to act in ways that *create* certain classes of social problems when they can make a profit doing so. Public policy making by business, in other words, helps create significant pieces of the agenda for public policy making by government. Society and government are forever trying to play catchup, to correct or mitigate the problems introduced by the technological and entrepreneurial ingenuity of the business sector.

Government's efforts are especially difficult because business executives

---

[8]See, for example, Jane Barker and Hazel Downing, "Word Processing and the Transformation of Patriarchal Relations of Control in the Office," pp. 147–64 in Donald MacKenzie and Judy Wajcman, eds., *The Social Shaping of Technology* (Philadelphia: Open University Press, 1985).

also are major participants in political life. The central role business plays in public policy making via the market gives it resources that can be used to intervene in the governmental side of public policy making, including funding much greater than that enjoyed by other social interests. As governments seek to induce businesses to reduce pollution, maintain good working conditions, and otherwise serve society, business executives and their allies possess considerable resources for resisting such efforts. The political role of business is a third central theme of the analysis in later chapters.

SOCIOECONOMIC AND POLITICAL INEQUALITY

A fourth structuring element in policy making is social and economic inequality among citizens and its translation into political inequalities. This occurs even in the political systems normally referred to as democracies.

The immediate or proximate decision makers in government, in business, and in the nonprofit sector comprise a small fraction of the citizenry. Perhaps half the industrial output and financial services of the United States are subject to primary control by the few thousand persons who make high-level decisions for the largest 500 corporations. There are even fewer top political officeholders: From 400 to 800 officials are elected to national office in Germany, Britain, and most other nations. A comparative handful of executives, editors, and journalism personnel decide what constitutes "news" at television networks, news-gathering organizations like the Associated Press, and major newspapers such as *The New York Times*. So, troubling as it may be, the existence of a decision-making elite—or, more accurately, elites—is a fact of political life.

Questions arise, however, concerning the extent to which such elites promote policy making that is democratic and intelligent. If elites were representative of the larger body of citizens, as by sharing ethnic background, religion, class, and gender, then their ideas and choices might not be too different from those of the public more generally. Even if unrepresentative in a demographic sense, if elites were highly responsive to public needs across a wide array of issues, and translated these into effective policy, many people might consider the system sufficiently democratic and intelligent. As we look into the matter, it will become apparent that such a pattern is not the norm.

Elites aside, issues of inequality reach further. Among ordinary citizens, donations to election campaigns obviously come from the affluent more than from the poor. Interest groups need funds, and they orient themselves to a degree toward those who supply the funding. In these and other ways, affluent people can draw on their economic resources when participating in political life. Nor do issues of inequality pertain to money alone, since writing and speaking abilities and many other personal traits favor some—and put others at a disadvantage.

Are contemporary political systems really not very democratic when it comes to equality, or can inequality somehow be squared with democracy? Are there political mechanisms at work to help soften the policy implications of the undeniable inequalities? To the extent that inequality is a problem, does it interfere with the degree of democracy only, or does it interfere also with the intelligence of public policy? These issues constitute the fourth central concern of the book.

HOW TO STUDY THE POLICY PROCESS?

What is the best way to examine the intricacies of policy making? A popular method in recent years separates policy making into its component steps and analyzes each in turn.[9] Such a step-by-step method begins with examination of how policy problems arise and first appear on the political agenda. There follows analysis of how political actors formulate issues for action, how legislative or other action ensues, how administrators subsequently implement the policy, and how policy is evaluated.

One quickly discovers, however, that the cast of characters in this drama does not change greatly in moving from the first act to the last. The ways in which political participants cooperate or struggle with each other also remain fairly consistent. Breaking up the policy-making process into hypothetical units is artificial, therefore, and also can entail great intellectual cost if searching for elements unique to each step obscures universal issues and phenomena, such as systematic inequalities that bias the entire process.[10]

The step-by-step approach also risks assuming that policy making proceeds through a coherent and rational process—like writing a term paper with a beginning, middle, and end, with each part tied logically to each succeeding part. In fact, policy making rarely proceeds in this manner; it has been described more accurately as resembling a "primeval soup," with action occurring fitfully as problems become matched with policy ideas considered to be in the political interests of a working majority of the partisans with influence over a policy domain.[11]

There may not even be a stage when problem definition occurs, since participants often vary widely in their ideas about "The Problem" a law or

---

[9]A thoughtful case for the step-by-step process can be found in James Anderson, *Public Policymaking: An Introduction* (Boston: Houghton Mifflin, 1990); for his rationale, see pp. 35–37.

[10]For a related critique of what she refers to as "an unexciting and unpersuasive 'production' model of policy, whereby policy is assembled in stages, as if on a conveyor belt," see Deborah A. Stone, *Policy Paradox and Political Reason* (Boston: Little Brown, 1988), pp. vii–viii and throughout.

[11]John W. Kingdon, *Agendas, Alternatives, and Public Policy* (Boston: Little Brown, 1984).

regulation is designed to serve. Policy sometimes is formed from a compromise among political participants, moreover, none of whom had in mind quite the problem to which the agreed policy responds. Action often springs from new opportunities, not from "problems" at all, as was true for space exploration.

Nor is it accurate to suggest that there is a certain step at which policy must be "decided." Keeping issues that would be inconvenient *off* the agenda is at least as important for political success as winning disputes that do arise.[12] Policy may emerge without any explicit decision, by failure to act. Policy may be an unintended byproduct of some other action: when the number of federal banking examiners was cut as a budgetary move in 1982–83, presumably no one intended it to enable shaky thrift institutions to get away with manipulating their financial records.[13] Or policy may emerge gradually, almost imperceptibly, via changes in how stringently a law is enforced.

Nor can implementation and evaluation reliably be distinguished from the other steps. An attempt to implement one policy almost always brings new problems onto the agenda, meaning that the step called *implementation* and the step called *agenda building* collapse into each other—as when the need to bail out failed savings and loan institutions arose in part because earlier revision of tax laws had encouraged real estate speculation. One group's solution often is another group's problem, as when less restrictive abortion laws galvanized antiabortion groups into action. From the seedbed of implementation, then, new policy problems grow and are plucked for the agenda in never-ending succession.[14]

Notice also that policy evaluation, often regarded as the end of the line, does not actually constitute a "step" in policy making unless it throws light on possible next moves in policy, in which case evaluation becomes intertwined with all other attempts to appraise and formulate options for reshaping government activity.

Deliberate, orderly steps therefore are not an accurate portrayal of how the policy process actually works. Policy making is, instead, a complexly interactive process without beginning or end. To make sense of it certainly requires attention to conventional governmental-political topics such as elections, elected functionaries, bureaucrats, and interest groups (see part II). But equally or more important are the deeper forces structuring and often distorting gov-

---

[12]See Peter Bachrach and Aryeh Botwinick, *Power and Empowerment: A Radical Theory of Participatory Democracy* (Philadelphia, PA: Temple University Press, 1992), especially "The Structural Mobilization of Bias," pp. 49–74.

[13]See Lawrence J. White, *The S&L Debacle: Public Policy Lessons for Bank and Thrift Regulation* (New York: Oxford University Press, 1991), pp. 88–90.

[14]In partial dissent from this view, Nelson W. Polsby argues that "political innovation in America is a phenomenon separable from other aspects of political life," in *Political Innovation in America* (New Haven, CT: Yale University Press, 1984), p. 172.

ernmental behavior: business influence, inequality, and impaired capacities for probing social problems. These intertwine in fascinating and disturbing ways in contemporary policy making (see part III). Some combination of modifying these structural conditions and reducing their distorting effects would need to be at the heart of any successful effort to make the policy-making process more intelligent and more democratic in the future (see part IV).

Chapter 2

The Limits of Analysis

The serious problems facing the world, together with the often disappointing performance of contemporary governments, seem to cry out for some better way of shaping social life. How can public policies be made more effective in actually solving social problems? Many people believe that the answer is to bring more information and systematic analysis into the policy-making process.

THE UBIQUITY OF ANALYSIS

How far do analysis and reasoned discussion go in policy making? In all political systems people gather facts, interpret them, and debate issues. Although these activities are often hurried and the results challenged or actually discarded, they are never absent. We need to appreciate the scope of current analytic efforts before investigating limits on their helpfulness, limits introduced both by the exercise of power and by inherent constraints on the capacity of thought to reach conclusive judgments about complex problems.

Elected functionaries and other officials, journalists, interest-group leaders, and concerned citizens often join in informed discussion on political issues, while specialized professional fact-finding, research, and policy analyses flourish as routine inputs into policy making. Since adversaries will deploy facts and arguments, a government functionary will ordinarily feel naked without help from both informed discussion and from specialized professional studies.

Even when partisan considerations press intensely, such as in deliberations regarding farm subsidies, a great deal of information is considered relevant. If wheat prices earned by farmers fall alarmingly, for example, the decline will be documented by the Department of Agriculture's far-flung statistical apparatus; agricultural economists and others will use the data to analyze causes and implications; and debate over what to do about the decline will raise many issues for discussion and perhaps for research. Why the decline? What price levels should be maintained? How does the decline (and attempts at restoration of price) affect the international balance of payments?

Decade by decade, governments enlarge the supply of systematic information and analysis brought to bear on policy making. An expanding array of monthly, quarterly, and annual statistical reports concern job creation and unemployment, price levels, imports and exports, morbidity and mortality rates, and many other subjects. In addition to such ongoing reports are more specialized endeavors, such as the Grace Commission on governmental effectiveness. Composed of task forces headed by 161 business executives, the commission produced a forty-seven–volume report for the president recommending 2,478 program and management changes intended to save $424 billion.[1]

Some government agencies are created partly or wholly to engage in analysis. In addition to its responsibilities for preparing the budget, for example, the Office of Management and Budget engages in numerous analytical tasks, including implementing President Reagan's famous Executive Order 12291, which required that each major new regulation issued by the executive branch pass a "regulatory impact analysis" showing that a regulation's benefits outweigh its costs.[2] The Congressional Budget Office provides a counterweight to economic and budgetary analyses conducted within the executive branch. The Congressional Research Service, General Accounting Office, and Office of Technology Assessment likewise serve Congress, publishing several thousand reports annually, as well as engaging in untold less formal interactions with legislators, their staffs, executive branch officials, interest groups, university professors, and many others. Many specialized research organizations established by or contracting with government agencies include the *Wissenschaftszentrum* in Berlin for German science and technology projects, Australia's Commission on the Future, and the RAND Corporation, originally created for strategic military research by the U.S. Air Force.

A kind of analysis sometimes called planning focuses on understanding

---

[1]Charles Goodsell, "The Grace Commission: Seeking Efficiency for the Whole People?," *Public Administration Review* 44 (May/June 1984): 62–82.

[2]This experience is reviewed in Peter M. Benda and Charles H. Levine, "Reagan and the Bureaucracy: The Bequest, the Promise, and the Legacy," pp. 102–142 in Charles O. Jones, ed., *The Reagan Legacy: Promise and Performance* (Chatham, NJ: Chatham House Publishers, 1988).

interrelations among policies in various areas or over time. Many local governments have planning and zoning commissions to analyze policies pertaining to land use. The U.S. President's Council of Economic Advisors provides advice regarding coordination of public policies on employment, price level, balance of payments, and economic growth. In Great Britain, the National Economic Development Council permits the government to achieve a more informed coordination of price, investment, employment, and foreign trade policies; the Commissariat du Plan performs a similar function in France; and the Japanese government's Ministry of International Trade and Industry (MITI) has become known as an exceptionally effective planning organization, sharing credit for the performance of the Japanese economy.

In a wealthy country like the United States, analysis pertinent to policy goes far beyond the studies conducted by government agencies. Numerous kinds of fact gathering, study, discussion, research, and processing of information pertinent to policy making altogether constitute a massive process engaging millions of persons and thousands of groups. Private corporations, interest groups, universities, and research institutions create a huge flow of unsolicited studies on policy. Thus, the Brookings Institution sponsors a dozen or more studies annually on government budgets, economic policy, military weaponry decisions, and many other topics from a moderately liberal perspective; and the American Enterprise Institute does the same from a mainstream conservative perspective.[3] Reagan administration policy was shaped in part on the basis of studies by the highly conservative Heritage Foundation.[4] Through books, articles, and a complex network of informal information interchange, even unaffiliated persons become important to the analysis of policy.[5] There runs a deep and wide river of information and opinion fed by many springs, from formal research projects to letters to the editor, some of which makes its way into the thinking of those with direct influence over policy. The flow of analysis is thinner in poor countries that cannot afford it, of course, and authoritarian governments stifle it.

LIMITS ON ANALYSIS AS A SUBSTITUTE FOR POLITICS

Why, given the obvious merits, do governments not make even more use of analysis? Why is there not less decision making on the basis of power and more on the basis of reasoned inquiry?

---

[3]James A. Smith, *The Idea Brokers: Think Tanks and the Rise of the New Policy Elite* (New York: The Free Press/Macmillan, 1991).

[4]For an illustrative example, see Stuart Butler, Michael Sanera, and Bruce Weinrod, eds., *Mandate for Leadership II* (Washington, DC: Heritage Foundation, 1984).

[5]Winning attention in the early 1990s, for example, was William Greider, *Who Will Tell the People?: The Betrayal of American Democracy* (New York: Simon & Schuster, 1992).

Perhaps there is an inadequate supply of fact, debate, and research in policy making. Yet available printed material on each of hundreds of policy problems, like science and math teaching, the Strategic Defense Initiative, or occupational retraining, runs to many thousands of pages—far in excess of what any elected functionary, administrator, or ordinary citizen has time to read. Thus, in a recent four-year period Congress received nearly 400 reports on energy policy, totalling some 20,000 pages, just from one source, the General Accounting Office. As a former presidential advisor said over three decades ago when the supply of information was a fraction of its current level, "Our policy makers do not lack advice; they are in many respects overwhelmed by it."[6]

Despite the overall quantity of information, the right kind of analysis often is not available for a problem at hand. A great deal of work by academic and other professional analysts is wasted in that government officials and citizens do not find what is offered them to be useful.[7] Conversely, researchers sometimes neglect subjects that turn out to be important. For example, the formerly communist nations are merely copying western-style political and economic systems instead of taking advantage of the social flexibility in eastern Europe to try out new political and economic arrangements, ones potentially superior to those now used anywhere in the world. Part of the reason is that European and American social scientists had not developed sufficiently detailed and helpful alternative ideas, and the proposals that were available (such as market socialism) were not well known or widely accepted.

Availability of information aside, what further limits are there on analysis? One way to find them is to undertake a thought experiment: try to imagine a situation in which information and reasoning alone would be sufficient to arrive at a policy conclusion. Could analysis ever complete the task of finding a solution for a complex policy problem?

Fallibility

To reach a solution without any exercise of power, sheer information and reasoning alone would have to be sufficient to bring all relevant parties into agreement. For unless they all are persuaded by the facts to accept the same policy outcome, their differences will have to be reconciled by power, by some political process such as voting.

A first obstruction to reasoned agreement is that any failures in logic by

---

[6]Henry A. Kissinger, *The Necessity for Choice* (New York: Harper & Row, Publishers, 1961), p. 351.

[7]On usable knowledge, see Charles E. Lindblom and David K. Cohen, *Usable Knowledge: Social Science and Social Problem Solving* (New Haven, CT: Yale University Press, 1979); and Edward J. Woodhouse, "Toward More Usable Technology Policy Analysis," in Gary Bryner, ed., *Science, Technology, and Politics: Policy Analysis in Congress* (Boulder, CO: Westview, 1992).

even one participant will bring the collectivity to disagreement. So would any significant differences in their available information. As long as such differences in fact and logic persist, analysis cannot settle their differences. Moreover, each person who does not himself or herself analyze the issues must *believe* in the infallibility of those who do. Otherwise, some people will reject the analysts' conclusions; and political means again would be necessary to reach a policy decision.

Yet ordinary citizens obviously are fallible, and so are experts and specialists. No educator fully understands how children with widely varying backgrounds and personalities should each be taught to read. Economists do not know enough to cope very well with simultaneous inflation and unemployment. Sociologists have a grossly incomplete understanding of social problems like drug abuse or criminal rehabilitation.

People in policy research and analysis themselves readily acknowledge their fallibility. As the first director of the Congressional Budget Office expressed it twenty years ago, "Considerable progress has been made in identifying and measuring social problems in our society, [and] systematic analysis has improved our knowledge of the distribution of the initial costs and benefits of social action programs." Yet, she adds, "little progress has been made in comparing the benefits of different social action programs, [and] little is known about how to produce more effective health, education, and other social services."[8]

Analysis also is fallible in more blatant ways in that much of it is poorly informed, superficial, or biased—not infrequently making shoddy attempts to prove by specious means what someone in power has already decided to think. Policy analysts also often blunder into tasks beyond their skills.[9] Even those in the policy analysis profession who sing its praises will acknowledge what they see as temporary limitations due to insufficiently developed analytical techniques.

The very best professional analysis never rises to infallibility. Some of the world's finest economists work as members or staff employees of the President's Council of Economic Advisors; but other excellent economists routinely challenge their findings, their theory, and their recommendations. A peculiar and not widely understood phenomenon in social analysis is that it often moves not toward agreement but spawns new questions with new disagreements. The famous Coleman report on the effect of school policies on student learning and achievement is illustrative: Although high-caliber sociologists,

[8]Alice M. Rivlin, *Systematic Thinking for Social Action* (Washington, DC: Brookings Institution, 1971), p. 7.

[9]On social scientists overreaching their limits and mistargeting their energies, see Lindblom and Cohen, 1979; and Charles E. Lindblom, *Inquiry and Change: The Troubled Attempt to Understand and Shape Society,* (New Haven, CT: Yale University Press, 1990), especially chapter 15.

psychologists, and other scholars spent $2 million on an assiduous study, its effect was to begin vast new controversies as additional complications were discovered in the relationship between school and learning.[10]

Too much and too little information.   An ordinary citizen, a government functionary, or a policy analyst who tries to grapple with the complexity of social problems is caught between the devil and the deep. On the one hand, he or she lacks sufficient information, not knowing what the consequences of one-way traffic might be, or "why Johnny can't read," or whether employment will rise or fall in the coming six months. Suppose, then, that an inquirer seeks further information. Long before acquiring what is needed, he or she will be overcome with more information than can be digested.

Many congressional practices can be understood as protections against this kind of information overload. Senators and Representatives have so little time to think about the hundreds of bills on the agenda that they end up specializing, largely following the lead of other members on problems outside their specialization.[11] Everyone who wants to think through a policy problem must steer a course between too little and too much information, but every path between the two is perilous.

Difficulties with using social analysis are all the greater because social problems and ways of thinking about them change. When economists began years ago to argue that governments could safely run deficits, that an unbalanced budget in government meant something quite different from an unbalanced budget for an individual or a business enterprise, the challenge of that view to "common sense" went beyond what many people could accept.[12] Just about the time that unbalanced budgets achieved the status of conventional wisdom early in the Reagan administration, quite a few economists began to warn about the need to cut swollen budget deficits—but others pooh-poohed the idea.

It is not surprising, therefore, that many people are confused about what to make of expert opinion. One often hears the complaint that lawmakers and citizens resist using the information and analysis available to them because they are ignorant, stubborn, or irrationally hostile to reasoned problem solving. Indeed, many sometimes are. Yet when one authority offers a finding or

---

[10]Compare James S. Coleman and others, *Equality of Educational Opportunity* (Washington, DC: U.S. Department of Health, Education, and Welfare, 1966) with Eric Hanushek and Lori Taylor, "Alternative Assessments of the Performance of Schools: Measurement of State Variations in Achievement," *Journal of Human Resources* 25 (1990):179–201.

[11]For a vivid, detailed account of how carefully a U.S. senator must allocate time to no more than a selected few policy problems, see Elizabeth Drew, *Senator* (New York: Simon & Schuster, 1979).

[12]The most perceptive skeptics perhaps perceived that the new advice did not actually rest on pure fact; rather it derived from a mixture of reasonably (but not conclusively) grounded empirical knowledge, together with certain professional norms or biases favored by economists.

recommendation on policy and another immediately disputes it, people often do not know whom to believe. When they cannot distinguish the good information from the bad, much of their resistance to factual claims reveals nothing more than wise skepticism.[13]

Conflict of Values

To make policy solely by analysis also would require a harmony of interests or values among all individuals and groups. If policies best for any one group also are best for all other social interests, there may be a chance of gaining universal assent to a proposed course of action. Otherwise, one group will gain while others lose, and why would the losers accept a policy disadvantageous to themselves?

Analysis rarely can find policies unequivocally good for all, of course; if beneficial for some groups, policies are likely to disadvantage others. Might the losers nevertheless be persuaded to accept the policy if their loss can be justified by some overriding criterion that everyone will accept? In principle, yes, but over 2,000 years of sophisticated philosophical inquiry have failed to produce an adequate criterion. How can we know the right distribution of income and wealth? What final criterion would justify building (or prohibiting) a plant to incinerate garbage, benefitting some people and harming others? How much should younger workers be taxed to subsidize medical costs of elderly retirees? Each person may have sensible answers to these questions, but established criteria that will achieve universal assent do not exist.[14]

Is majority will the answer? Many people would endorse the idea that majority views sometimes should prevail over what a minority wants. But no one holds to such a principle for all cases—such as enslaving or taking all the assets of a minority for the benefit of a majority. In fact, on close inspection, the majority criterion holds just in special cases, and some people flatly deny the virtue of the criterion altogether.

The public interest criterion. Does the concept of the public interest provide a criterion for policy analysis?[15] Sometimes *public interest* refers to some universal good, to certain values believed to serve everyone. So you may say,

---

[13]On social or cultural rationality, contrasted with expert advice, see Charles Perrow, *Normal Accidents: Living with High-Risk Technologies* (New York: Basic Books, 1984), pp. 315–16, 321–24; and Joseph G. Morone and Edward J. Woodhouse, *The Demise of Nuclear Energy? Lessons for Democratic Control of Technology* (New Haven, CT: Yale University Press, 1989), pp. 134–35.

[14]For an illuminating discussion of this problem in public choice theory, see Russell Hardin, "Constitutional Political Economy: Agreement on Rules," *British Journal of Political Science* 18 (October 1988):513–30.

[15]On the concept and problems with it, see Bruce Douglass, "The Common Good and the Public Interest," *Political Theory* 8 (1980):103–17.

"Air pollution control serves the public interest," meaning that pollution harms not just you but many other people as well and that gains from controlling it would be worth the cost. But what if others do not agree with you? Who adjudicates disputes over what is in the public interest?

⁂ The eighteenth-century utilitarian Jeremy Bentham thought he had found in the principle "the greatest good for the greatest number" a criterion for policy analysis on which agreement should be possible. The egalitarian spirit of his principle was not universally acceptable, since some people oppose equality. In addition, his principle proved logically defective, for the greatest good cannot simultaneously be given to the greatest number: To give maximum benefits to one person ordinarily requires withholding some from others.

Responding to this technical difficulty, economists have explored the possibility that maximization of total utility (or satisfaction) in society might be a universally acceptable criterion. The best policy, some proposed, would be one that created the largest amount of "want-satisfaction." But this principle likewise proves defective on many counts. Most people do not believe that want-satisfaction is always acceptable as a goal; they think some wants ought not to be satisfied—such as for hallucinogenic drugs or abortions. Others may prefer some specific distribution of want-satisfaction, such as in favor of those who work hard, or Brahmins, or whites, or whoever. It is not necessary to endorse such views to note that they cannot be wished away.

Despite these difficulties, there is a fair amount of agreement on grand principles like "Everyone who wants to work deserves to have a job." The insuperable problem for analysis arises at a more concrete level: To reduce unemployment by a small percentage, is it worth risking an increase in the rate of inflation? Ought taxes to be raised enough to pay an extra $1 billion for job training programs? Cost-benefit and other calculations can provide insights on such tradeoffs, but analysis inevitably fails to add up to *one clearcut answer* that will be compelling to all persons and groups with differing values.

Time and Cost

Analysis also runs afoul of the necessity that it be completed in the time and with the resources available. This is an impossible hope for sufficiently complex problems, especially in overworked and underfunded governmental agencies, or when studies are conducted at the deliberate pace typical of university-based social research. Most policy decisions are made using no more than perfunctory analysis, because decisions cannot wait until "all the facts are in." Sustained analysis requires not hours or weeks, but months or years. Biological and social scientists have now been working for at least three decades, expending hundreds of millions of dollars annually in recent years, researching cancer risks; but respected members of the research community are nowhere near agreement on such fundamental matters as whether testing on mice can be reliably extrapolated to humans, whether removing asbestos from schools is a good idea, or whether synthetic chemicals pose a significant risk compared with naturally occurring chemical substances.[16]

Because analysis takes time, it eats up resources. During each day a government functionary must make many decisions, so he or she could quickly exhaust the budget by turning problems into extended research projects. Each major study undertaken by the Office of Technology Assessment, for example, costs nearly a million dollars—and these studies are neither comprehensive nor conclusive.[17] Because analysis is in any case fallible, the public official will often wisely refuse to invest heavily in it.[18] No government has yet financed a massive, near-conclusive research project on any complex policy choice, even as an experiment to see how much it would cost to do so; costs are perceived to be too high relative to the expected value of the resulting product.

Most policy questions therefore are decided by faster, cheaper methods than by analysis: most commonly, by delegating responsibility for decisions to designated officials who must decide, drawing on whatever information is available.

Problem Formulation

Finally, analysis could eliminate the need for politics only if, in addition to all the aforementioned conditions, the very definition of society's problems could be made analytically. Otherwise, disputes over which problems to attack would call for a political settlement.

Policy makers do not face a given problem, not even a given set of problems. Instead they must identify and formulate each of their problems. When riots break out in Los Angeles, what is the "real" problem: decline of law and order? racial and ethnic discrimination? poverty and joblessness? family disintegration? poor police training? And what are the causes of these problems?

Although analysis can help in reaching sensible judgments on all such questions, it cannot provide full answers to any of them. At some point, the question of how to formulate a problem calls for an act of choice or will. Some ways to formulate complex social problems surely are more useful than others in a given situation, but there never is a single, clearly correct problem

---

[16]Aaron Wildavsky, *Searching for Safety* (New Brunswick, NJ: Transaction Books, 1988); Philip H. Abelson, "Exaggerated Carcinogenicity of Chemicals," *Science* 256 (June 19, 1992):1609.

[17]To appreciate just how far away from being conclusive a typical study is, see U.S. Congress Office of Technology Assessment, *Trade and Environment: Conflicts and Opportunities* (Washington, DC: USGPO 052–003–01282–1, May 1992).

[18]For a systematically skeptical view of the value of advice in decision making, see David Collingridge and Colin Reeve, *Speaking Truth to Power: The Role of Experts in Policy Making* (London: Frances Pinter, 1985).

definition on which analysis can converge. Nor is there any purely analytic way of specifying which problems, once formulated, ought to be higher than others on the political agenda.[19] Such judgments, moreover, contain moral components; so the issues cannot be fully settled except by reference to values or interests in conflict in any society. The settlement requires politics more than analysis.

CONCLUSION

In short, analytical policy making is inevitably limited—and must allow room for politics—to the degree that

1. It is fallible, and people believe it to be so.
2. It cannot wholly resolve conflicts of value and interests.
3. It is too slow and costly.
4. It cannot tell us conclusively which problems to attack.

Hence, there is no realistic prospect of substituting analysis for political interaction on any wholesale basis; and efforts in that direction are misguided, even dangerously misleading.[20]

This line of inquiry has rich implications for the role of experts in policy making. If professional analysis deserves to be seen as no more than an input to political interaction and judgment, never a substitute for it, then inquiry and judgment by ordinary people remain at the heart of the policy-making process.

It may nevertheless be possible for professional analysis to become more helpful for political decision making. But efforts in that direction need to be approached in ways that respect the limits of analysis and that adapt analysis to the needs of ordinary citizens and of political functionaries. Later chapters take up that task.

First, however, chapter 3 examines how democratic political interaction has the potential to evolve sensible policy in circumstances where analysis alone cannot.

---

[19]On problem formulation and agenda setting, see Nelson Polsby, *Political Innovation in America* (New Haven, CT: Yale University Press, 1984); and John W. Kingdon, *Agendas, Alternatives, and Public Policies* (Boston: Little Brown, 1984).

[20]For an early critique of the tendency to attempt to substitute analysis for political interaction, see Charles E. Lindblom, "The Science of 'Muddling Through,'" *Public Administration Review* 19 (1959):79–88. Efforts to carve out a larger, but still feasible, role for analysis include John Dryzek, "Complexity and Rationality in Public Life," *Political Studies* 35 (1987):424–42.

Chapter *3*

The Potential Intelligence
of Democracy

If complex social problems cannot be solved through analysis for all the reasons discussed in chapter 2, then shaping a better world will depend largely on the extent to which political arrangements evoke fair and sensible judgments. This poses a fundamental puzzle, early articulated by Plato: How can government be organized to locate power and wisdom in the same place?

Democratic politics aspires to solve this conundrum by making office holders responsive to the collective wisdom of the citizenry. Yet even cursory inspection of political debates and governmental actions reveals that humanity has a long way to go in learning to bring into alignment power, wisdom, and responsiveness to the public. Nevertheless, comparison of democratic political systems with the sorry state of most nondemocratic nations—epitomized by the condition of the former Soviet Union—suggests that there may be some underlying rationality or intelligence in democratic processes, even ones that remain seriously flawed. Of what does this virtue consist?

It does not rest in freedoms of speech, press, and other civil liberties per se, since even a very free society might be unable to organize to solve its problems. Nor can the success of democracy be explained primarily by the phenomenon of elections: Some nations like Mexico have regular elections without very successful policy making; some elected leaders, such as Hitler, overthrow their democratic systems. And even if elections guaranteed sensible and successful government, we would need to ask what enables them to do so.

Partially obscured by the more obvious features of democratic politics are certain intelligence-enhancing processes and strategies. These strategies are not presently used nearly well enough, and serious social problems go unresolved decade after decade. But to the extent that democratic systems do work, it is largely because they half-wittingly utilize strategies that render complex social problems far more manageable than could be achieved via analysis alone.

AGREEMENT IN LIEU OF COMPLETE UNDERSTANDING

Democratic systems set up processes by which political participants *interact* with each other to formulate policy. Such interactions produce more intelligent outcomes under many circumstances than highly analytical methods can. In a way, this is a very familiar idea, an extension of the notion that two heads are better than one. Yet the claim that democracy is intelligent is also a bit weird, since everyone knows how poorly governments often perform. Participants in political life not infrequently put their own good ahead of the good of others; and many citizens and elected officials seem relatively ignorant about the issues being debated. So how can the whole hodgepodge of them possibly produce intelligent outcomes?

The benefits of democracy arise in no small part from the fact that interactive policy making copes with many of the difficulties that analysis cannot, including limits on human time, energy, and understanding. To grasp this requires a step-by-step thinking through of what happens when people with different outlooks and priorities have to reach agreement with each other.

Partisanship

Many citizens, perhaps especially students in courses about politics, decry what they see as the biases of decision makers, and they place the blame for political failures on narrow-minded individuals serving special interests at the expense of the public good. They believe that to get politics working again we need people who are willing to "be objective," to make decisions based on "the facts." Even among policy professionals one sometimes finds "a profound rejection of politics in favor of rational analysis."[1] As chapter 2 makes apparent, however, there is no possibility of replacing politics by analysis. So while acknowledging that many politicians are not sufficiently open-minded, thoughtful, and public-spirited, we need to inquire whether these shortcomings inevitably prevent sensible policy making.

Political participants all are partisans—that is, they do not share a domi-

---

[1]Deborah A. Stone, *Policy Paradox and Political Reason* (Boston: Little Brown, 1988), p. vii.

nant common purpose; instead, each pursues some combination of private purposes and his or her own vision of the public interest. Fortunately, it turns out that by interacting with each other, such partisans often can work out ways for many of them to get at least some of what they need.[2]

How does this occur? Because of the shortcomings of analysis, there is no way to calculate the "correct" approach to a complex policy issue. There is no way analytically to set the agenda regarding which problems are to be taken up, nor even to define what "the problems" are. But individuals and organizations are perfectly willing to *declare* what they take to be the high-priority problems and to propose solutions. Such proposals sometimes are plausibly justified but never are fully proven superior to other possible problem definitions, agendas, and policy options. Fortunately, proof is unnecessary: Action is undertaken not when a policy option is proven correct, but when a working majority of those with influence over an issue reach agreement with each other—as happens not infrequently between President Clinton and fellow Democrats in Congress.

Mere agreement seems too flimsy a basis for policy making; it is a necessary expedient, perhaps, but can it really be considered an intelligent way to run a society? To evaluate that, one needs some way of judging what constitutes an "intelligent" political process. No one has a definitive set of criteria for that, but many people might look for at least the following:

1. That concerns moderately or strongly held by any sizeable number of people are taken into account in some nontrivial way;
2. That reasonable tradeoffs are made among conflicting values; and
3. That, insofar as feasible, policy actions take into account available information about social problems and opportunities, performance of existing programs, costs, and other relevant matters.

Although no political system presently is designed to achieve these elements of intelligent policy making nearly as well as can be envisioned, it turns out that negotiations and other adjustments among political partisans often can achieve a measure of all these goals. How does this happen?

Search for Agreement

Consider some of the ways partisans are likely to think about making and responding to policy proposals:[3]

1. In crafting a proposal, partisans will tend to look for ways to get what they want without stirring up adverse responses or retaliations from others. So the search

---

[2]How many get how much of what they need varies greatly, of course, depending in part on how widely power over a policy is shared, as discussed in subsequent chapters.

[3]These ideas are developed more precisely and in greater detail in Charles E. Lindblom, *The Intelligence of Democracy: Decision Making Through Mutual Adjustment* (New York: The Free Press, 1965), especially pp. 205–45.

for agreement simultaneously becomes a method of taking diverse views into account.

2. Knowing that they will need allies when putting forth their own proposals, others are disposed to grant what proposers ask unless there is some good reason not to do so. Thus, a bias toward action is built into the system: I'll help you get what you need, if you'll help me get what I need.

3. Those with initial objections have strong motivation to come up with counterproposals, ones that will allow them to join with the original proposer in seeking a mutually beneficial outcome.

4. The need to win agreement keeps demands within the sphere likely to be considered "reasonable" or intelligent by most of those whose agreement is needed.

5. Moderation likewise is encouraged because those putting forth a proposal will be wasting their own scarce time, energy, and other resources if they cannot win agreement; and, even if eventually winnable, immoderate proposals may not be worth the effort—and the favors used up in the process.

Working in these ways for their own private gain and for their own vision of the public interest, partisans interact with each other in ways that often converge toward fairly sensible outcomes. The need to achieve agreement leads to policy making that, to some degree, aims for the three goals of responsiveness to public sentiment, sensible tradeoffs, and attention to relevant information.

These interactions can be thought of as *substituting* politics for analysis. No one really "understands" the social problem that (hopefully) is being ameliorated, since the participants each hold somewhat different definitions of what the problem is. Thus, when President Bush changed his stance in mid 1992 and supported extension of unemployment compensation benefits, he presumably was thinking partly about the problem of how to win re-election; but this did not prevent him from reaching agreement with liberal senators who were primarily concerned with helping unemployed workers who had exhausted their benefits. What they all agreed on was not the definition of a problem, but on a program that a working majority considered superior to the existing policy.

Alternatively, with equal justification we might say that political interaction *achieves* a form of understanding that cannot be produced through analysis alone. Since understanding generally is sought as a means to improved action, whenever a working majority agrees on a new or revised policy, that policy can be thought of as embodying a new understanding. This accords with one definition of the term *understanding*: a shared agreement.

Under either of these interpretations, partisan interaction helps reach agreement on policies even when it is not possible to fully analyze and understand the issues at stake.

STRATEGIC ANALYSIS

As partisans interact, they also analyze—some more or better than others, of course. And they often do so strategically, getting around the limits to analysis discussed in chapter 2. Among the strategies common in democratic politics are those discussed below, all of which help to simplify and focus.

Simple Incremental Analysis

Political participants often limit themselves to considering policies fairly close to the status quo. Because it usually is impossible to win agreement on large changes, restricting analysis to "incremental" policy proposals that may be politically feasible is a way of conserving on scarce time and energy.[4]

Focusing on small variations from present policy also makes the most of available knowledge: Because the new options are not terribly different from present and past policies, a great deal of what administrators and other participants already know about existing programs will be applicable to evaluating the new proposals. While uncertainty may still be substantial, errors probably will be smaller. The economic effects of a 10-cent or even a 50-cent hike in the gas tax obviously are easier to understand than the consequences of a nearly total shift in energy usage.

Critics of incremental analysis are concerned that it is a conservative process, that it will maintain the status quo and not work well for those who want to change society, tending "to neglect *basic* societal innovations."[5] It would be indefensible for a society to think only about small changes, of course; we would fail to begin preparing policy ideas for the future, and could default on addressing serious social problems requiring substantial change.[6]

Considering the potential magnitude of the climate warming that could result from burning fossil fuels that release carbon dioxide, it is important for some scholars and environmental activists to develop radical proposals for energy conservation, coupled with drastic shifts away from fossil fuels and toward renewable energy sources. But since a major energy reorientation is politically infeasible at present, it also makes sense for many political participants to focus on smaller changes, such as higher gasoline taxes, increased subsidies for mass transit, and greater encouragement for car pooling.[7]

If problems are considered sufficiently severe, partisans seeking change have a choice between pressing for immediate radical reforms or seeking to make many smaller steps in a relatively short period. The latter is often—but

[4]This long-practiced strategy was systematically analyzed in Charles E. Lindblom, "The Science of 'Muddling Through'," *Public Administration Review* 19 (1959):79–88.

[5]Amitai Etzioni, "Mixed Scanning: A 'Third' Approach to Decision-Making," *Public Administration Review* 27 (1967):385–92. Also see Amitai Etzioni, "Mixed Scanning Revisited," *Public Administration Review* 46 (1986):8–15. A recent, balanced appraisal is Michael T. Hayes, *Incrementalism and Public Policy* (New York: Longman, 1992).

[6]On the problem of small steps, see Paul R. Schulman, *Large-Scale Policy Making* (New York: Elsevier, 1980); Michael A. H. Dempster and Aaron Wildavsky, "There is No Magic Size for an Increment," *Political Studies* 27 (1979):371–89; and R. Goodin and I. Waldner, "Thinking Big, Thinking Small, and Not Thinking at All," *Public Policy* 27 (1979):1–24.

[7]Policy options for addressing climate warming ranging from mild to radical are in Joseph I. Lieberman, "To Market, To Market," *Issues in Science and Technology* VII (Summer 1992):25–29, and Christopher Flavin, "Building a Bridge to Sustainable Energy," pp. 27–45 in Lester R. Brown et al., *State of the World 1992* (New York: W. W. Norton, 1992).

not always—both more feasible politically and more prudent analytically than leaping well beyond the limits of understanding.[8]

Focus on a Few Policy Options

A closely related strategy is to focus on a handful of policy alternatives rather than trying to be comprehensive. Of course this may lead to neglect of some attractive policy options. But partisans can be relied on to propose those few options they consider most suitable, all things considered. This is very far from a guarantee of finding a policy that combines political feasibility and successful problem solving; but considering that approximately a thousand pieces of legislation are introduced annually in the U.S. Congress, it is vital to have some sensible way of targeting scarce time and energy. Limiting serious attention to a manageable number of alternatives meets that requirement.

Focus Mostly on Ills to Be Remedied

Does thoughtful policy require policy makers to formulate an organized set of policy aspirations, or should they focus merely on ameliorating the most pressing problems? The latter often is a more sensible tack. It is too hard—analytically as well as in terms of achieving political agreement—to specify positive targets for various dates in the future for all the goals connected with a complex area of public policy. In the case of housing, for example, such targets could include

1. A specified number of housing units available within a given price range;
2. Creation of a determined number of jobs within a given salary range, to make sure each person can afford housing;
3. Psychological research, mental health programs, and whatever else would be required to assure that each person has the necessary faculties to hold a job and take care of a home;
4. Goals for education and job training, to ensure that each person has the skills necessary to hold a job;
5. All the social rearrangements necessary to produce people with personalities and behaviors that will lead them away from addiction to drugs or alcohol, which sometimes prevents holding a job and may lead to homelessness; and
6. Plans to integrate housing so that Caucasians, Hispanics, Asians, African-Americans, and others can live together harmoniously.

---

[8]There has been little sustained analysis of the relative advantages and disadvantages of the two options. Compare Charles E. Lindblom, "Still Muddling, Not Yet Through," *Public Administration Review* 39 (1979):517–26; Ian Lustick, "Explaining the Variable Utility of Disjointed Incrementalism: Four Propositions," *American Political Science Review* 74 (1980):342–53; Jennifer L. Hochschild, *The New American Dilemma: Liberal Democracy and School Desegregation* (New Haven, CT: Yale University Press, 1984); Grover Starling, "Making Strategic Decisions in High-Technology Environments," *Policy Sciences* 24 (1991):227–43; and Hayes, *Incrementalism and Public Policy*.

Instead of the utopian task of planning a nation's housing and then planning all the political, economic, and social control processes that would be necessary to implement the plans, participants in policy making almost always limit themselves to a much simpler method of dealing with housing policy: Attack egregious ills (or move toward especially promising opportunities). Thus, shelters for homeless people were expanded greatly (though not enough) to ameliorate one of the worst housing problems of the 1980s. When blacks faced housing discrimination in the 1960s and 1970s, fair housing laws and new court interpretations made it harder to discriminate against minorities. To help bring down the expense of owning a home, interest paid on mortgages is tax deductible, a subsidy of several hundred dollars monthly for each middle-class homeowner. Numerous other particular programs nibble at small pieces of the huge domain of housing policy.

Should there be better housing policies? Certainly. But it is by no means clear that aiming at a comprehensive, utopian housing policy would make things any better. It is hard enough to figure out what can be done for mentally ill people who are homeless, to win agreement from politicians and taxpayers to pay for the necessary programs, and then to administer such programs successfully. Would a broader, more visionary aim stand much chance of being translated into effective action?

Trial and Error

A fourth strategy for making social problems more comprehensible is to approach them through a sequence of policy moves using trials, errors, and revised trials. Policy making thus is a never-ending process rather than a once-and-for-all settling of issues. Especially in U.S. government, but to some degree in policy making everywhere, one returns again and again to reconsider issues; budget deficits, abortion, military weaponry procurement, and leasing of federal lands for oil exploration are among dozens of issues recurring on the political agenda.

All participants in policy making are condemned to such serial reconsideration, and many come to expect it and think of it as good strategy. Trial and error fits with the strategies for making incremental changes in policy, sharply reducing the number of alternative policies to be explored, and reducing the number and complexity of factors to be analyzed. Returning time after time to a set of issues helps government functionaries to become familiar with problems and programs, potentially allowing them to develop enough feel for an issue to ask probing questions about it. Attention can focus on what is politically feasible at a given time, expecting that underemphasized aspects of the problem can be dealt with at a later time if political circumstances allow.

Trial and error is not simply a means of pursuing the other strategies previously introduced, however. It is an independently justifiable strategy, simplifying and focusing otherwise unmanageably complex problems by allowing experience to help fill in what human foresight cannot supply. Trial-and-error learning is by no means an easy, automatic process (see chapter 11). Errors can and do accumulate and proliferate, instead of being corrected. There will usually be disagreement about whether an "error" has occurred, what exactly the error is, what its causes are, and what an "error correction" should look like.[9] Nevertheless, by monitoring feedback from experience, sufficient insight may be gained gradually to shape revised and improved policy trials.[10]

FRAGMENTATION OF ANALYSIS AMONG PARTISANS

Although it is crucial to use various strategies for whittling down problems to a manageable size, the inevitable result is that individual political participants, government agencies, and interest groups will neglect important considerations outside the scope of their immediate pursuits. Fortunately, democratic political systems have an implicit strategy for coping with this problem as well: Rather than relying on any one set of analysts or partisans to attend to every issue in superhuman fashion, different people become watchdogs for different social problems and needs.

For any given problem, moreover, various groups will attend to somewhat different aspects of the issue, producing different kinds of information as their contributions to political interaction. For cleanup of hazardous waste dumps, for example, community groups may do informal door-to-door surveys of health symptoms,[11] local governments may test water samples, a state environmental agency may conduct research on the businesses responsible for dumping the waste, and the federal Environmental Protection Agency may study chemical compounds at the site and evaluate whether the site belongs on the Superfund list for federally funded cleanup.

This division of labor deserves to be underlined. Many advocates of more analysis and less politics in public policy making have simply taken for

---

[9]On barriers to learning from experience, see Joseph G. Morone and Edward J. Woodhouse, *Averting Catastrophe: Strategies For Regulating Risky Technologies* (Berkeley: University of California Press, 1986).

[10]On feedback as an aid to decision making see Karl Deutsch, *The Nerves of Government* (New York: The Free Press, 1966); John D. Steinbruner, *The Cybernetic Theory of Decision* (Princeton, NJ: Princeton University Press, 1974); and David Collingridge, *Critical Decision Making: A New Theory of Social Choice* (New York: St. Martin's Press, 1982).

[11]The indispensability of analysis by ordinary citizens was made clear at Love Canal, where housewife Lois Gibbs understood the dangers early on. As she later put it, after becoming director of the Citizens Clearinghouse for Hazardous Waste, professional environmentalists often are concerned with middle-of-the-road regulatory fine-tuning and "do not want to tackle any issue that challenges the fundamental, cozy relationships between industry and government." Quoted in Bruce Piasecki and Peter Asmus, *In Search of Environmental Excellence* (New York: Simon & Schuster, 1990), p. 151.

granted that analysis should always be placed at the service of some government functionary who has comprehensive responsibilities in a problem area. But there is no such person, because each official deals at any given time with limited problems, within a limited perspective.

Consider a representative of a municipal health department serving on an interdepartmental committee charged with recommending a location for a new high school. If the health officer sees her role as finding the best location, her analytical tasks would be extremely large and varied—indeed, impossible since there is no one location best in every respect. In fact, however, she is likely to construe her role as attending primarily to the bearing of the school's location on health—and of persuading the other committee members from traffic, police, education, fire, zoning, and budget that health considerations are relevant. In that case, her analytical tasks are reduced to a much narrower range.

When politics succeeds it is precisely because responsibilities are divided so that each participant usefully *can* play a limited role. Each speaks for some few angles on a complex problem, with the interplay of ideas and suggestions from diverse participants representing a fuller range of relevant considerations. This is no guarantee of a "good" policy, of course: Some participants may play their roles poorly, leaving crucial considerations badly represented; inequalities in power may give disproportionate weight to certain considerations; and some relevant views may go wholly unrepresented. But the limited role played by each political participant does make the analytic task at least feasible, a prerequisite to helpfulness.

Overall, as the diversity of those participating influentially in policy making increases, the number of important considerations neglected will decrease, because social needs neglected by one group or agency will tend to be taken up by another. There rarely is nearly *enough* diversity in democratic political systems as presently set up, and some issues are badly neglected year after year, a point we consider at some length in later chapters. But there is more diversity in these systems—hence better protection of a wider range of social needs—than in nondemocratic polities. And the fragmentation of responsibility among many partisan interest groups, agencies, and issue entrepreneurs—coupled with the other strategies—does have a focusing and simplifying effect on issues that otherwise would be hopelessly complex.

CONCLUSION

Strategic analysis and mutual adjustment among political participants, then, are the underlying processes by which democratic systems achieve the level of intelligent action that they do. Bewilderingly complex social problems become manageable—when they do—by these methods.

There is never a point at which the thinking, research, and action is "objective," or "unbiased." It is partisan through and through, as are all human activities, in the sense that the expectations and priorities of those commissioning and doing the analysis shape it, and in the sense that those using information shape its interpretation and application.

Information seeking and shaping must intertwine inextricably with political interaction, judgment, and action. Since time and energy and brainpower are limited, strategic analysis must focus on those aspects of an issue that participating partisans consider to be most important for persuading each other. There is no purely analytical way to do such focusing, it requires political judgments: about what the crucial unknowns are, about what kind of evidence is likely to be persuasive to would-be allies, or about what range of alternatives may be politically feasible. In this sense, what are usually called biases actually can be helpful, since they provide a way of focusing analysis and action.

Those who advocate more rational problem solving see incrementalism and the other strategies as indecisive, makeshift, timid, narrow, inconclusive, and procrastinating. They fear that "adversarial stalemate, paralysis, and drift are as likely as problem amelioration" and worry that political participants could "cross and recross intersections without knowing where we were going."[12] That is indeed the case. But the alternative to strategic analysis and action is even less defensible: Waiting to act in a complex situation until one understands the consequences is a prescription for paralysis. In comparison, thoughtful trial and error and the other strategies look fairly good.[13]

This happy coincidence between democratic practice and intelligent decision making is indeed good news, and it is a story that humanity at least dimly understands, as demonstrated by the enormous hunger for democracy in the nations where it has for so long been suppressed by dictatorial regimes. Unfortunately, there is a darker side to democratic governance, one that threatens the achievement in practice of what is feasible in principle. Poverty, crime, arms races, waste of energy resources, pollution, and many other problems obviously have gone on for decades or centuries; so it would be silly to think that actual practice presently comes very close to the potential intelligence achievable through democratic interaction and strategic analysis. Chapters 4 through 7 analyze ways that conventional political institutions both promote and interfere with intelligent, democratic interaction among partisans. Later chapters consider how democratic political interaction could be improved to produce wiser policy, in part by developing a more intelligent form of trial and error (see Part IV).

---

[12]John Dryzek, "Complexity and Rationality in Public Life," *Political Studies* 35 (1987):424–42, quote from p. 435; and John Forester, "Bounded Rationality and the Politics of Muddling Through," *Public Administration Review* 44 (1984):23–31, quote from p. 23.

[13]An extended review and appraisal of the critics' positions, together with a suggested reformulation, is in Andrew Weiss and Edward J. Woodhouse, "Reframing Incrementalism: A Constructive Response to the Critics," *Policy Sciences* 25 (1992).

PART II

CONVENTIONAL GOVERNMENT AND POLITICS

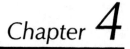

The Imprecision of Voting

If ordinary citizens are to help produce intelligent and democratic policy outcomes, they must join in the complex processes of partisan interaction outlined in chapter 3. Elections are usually considered one of the main mechanisms through which this occurs. To understand what goes right and wrong with citizen participation in policy making, therefore, one must understand what elections are and are not good for.

Do voters determine policy indirectly via their votes for elected representatives? If so, obstacles to intelligent, democratic policy making would be due almost exclusively to defects in electoral processes, to shortcomings in voters' competence and interest in political matters, and to manipulation of voters. A sharply contrasting view among many political scientists is that voters only get to choose among competing would-be rulers.[1] The vote typically permits citizens to decide *who* will make policy, this view alleges, but does not actually give them other significant influence *over policy.*

Citizens in France, Japan, the United States, and throughout the world do not usually vote directly for policies—except occasionally when a few issues are decided through referenda. Does this mean that citizens surrender all sig-

---

[1]See Joseph Schumpeter, *Capitalism, Socialism, and Democracy,* 3rd ed. (New York: Harper & Row, Publishers, 1949), chapter 22; and Thomas R. Dye and L. Harmon Zeigler, *The Irony of Democracy,* 8th ed. (Pacific Grove, CA: Brooks/Cole, 1990).

nificant influence on policy? Clearly not: Elected officials read and respond to mail from their constituents, and candidates for office to some degree tailor their policy commitments to suit voters. Citizens also influence policy through interest-group activity, some of which involves campaign financing and endorsement.[2] Just how much control over policy do ordinary citizens attain via the vote and other activities associated with electoral politics? And to what extent are deficiencies in policy making due to electoral mechanisms and other aspects of the voting process?

LOOSENESS OF CONTROL

Some 80 percent of the American public expressed support for a freeze on numbers of nuclear weapons in the early 1980s, just when the Reagan administration embarked on a substantial buildup of strategic arms. A similar discrepancy arose regarding the administration's support of the Contras in Nicaragua, with polls showing most Americans opposed to intervention there despite their perception of communism as a threat in Central America.[3]

Large majorities favor expanding day-care facilities for working parents, arranging productive work for able-bodied recipients of public assistance, and generally developing jobs for those who want to work. Yet the U.S. government has not been very active in providing jobs since the New Deal, despite "no shortage of work-related proposals for dealing with the problems faced and posed by the underclass."[4]

A majority of Americans consistently favored the Equal Rights Amendment after its approval by Congress in 1972, yet it failed to achieve ratification by three quarters of the states by the ten-year deadline in 1982.[5] Majority support proved insufficient, because the Constitution is virtually impossible to amend over the opposition of a strong minority.

More generally, studies that track opinion and policy change on hundreds of issues over decades suggest that policy fails to correspond with public opinion at least one third of the time.[6] Whether these discrepancies necessarily

---

[2]In all nations, policy makers take some account of what citizens need and want, regardless of whether there are electoral or other channels for citizen influence, because failing to do so may lead to insurrection, a listless workforce, or other difficulties that even dictators want to avoid.

[3]Richard Sobel, "Public Opinion About United States Intervention in El Salvador and Nicaragua," *Public Opinion Quarterly* 53 (Spring 1989):114–28, quote from p. 114.

[4]Robert Y. Shapiro et al., "Employment and Social Welfare," *Public Opinion Quarterly* 51 (Summer 1987):268–81, quote from pp. 268–69.

[5]Jane J. Mansbridge, *Why We Lost the ERA* (Chicago: University of Chicago Press, 1986); Gilbert Y. Steiner, *Constitutional Inequality: The Political Fortunes of the Equal Rights Amendment* (Washington, DC: Brookings, 1985).

[6]Robert Y. Shapiro and Lawrence R. Jacobs, "The Relationship Between Public Opinion and Public Policy: A Review," pp. 149–79 in *Political Behavior Annual,* vol. II, Samuel Long, ed. (Boulder, CO: Westview, 1989).

point to a flaw in the policy-making process is debatable. Almost everyone believes in delegation of considerable authority to elected officials, and it should not be surprising if representatives sometimes reach judgments differing from those of their constituents. Still, those advocating greater popular control of policy making can question the legitimacy of such significant and enduring discrepancies as those now prevailing. What attributes of the voting process make it difficult to translate majority viewpoints into public policy?

Voter Ignorance of Candidate Positions

Many citizens know little about the candidates, with about one third of American adults not recognizing the name of the incumbent from their district in the House of Representatives. Only one in seven of those who recognized the incumbent's name claimed to remember his or her vote on even a single piece of legislation—and some of them were mistaken. So only a small fraction of the citizenry is equipped to reward or punish representatives on the basis of particular policy choices.[7]

Might there nevertheless be loose control on the basis of incumbents' general voting records? Approximately one third of all adults in the United States (but half of all voters) have at least a vague idea of their representative's general political stance on the liberal-conservative continuum. This would be enough to influence the outcome of many reelection races, except that

> not everyone with the requisite knowledge votes on the basis of policy distance from the incumbent. People may cast their votes for any number of other reasons, ranging from how honest to how photogenic the incumbent is. Deference to the incumbent, party loyalty, personal loyalty, or lack of an attractive alternative may lead people to vote to reelect regardless of how distant the representative's policies are from their own.[8]

For presidential candidates, however, there is a clearer perception of where candidates stand. For example, two thirds of voters correctly perceived that Dukakis was more liberal than Bush in 1988 on such issues as aid to minorities, domestic spending, and national health insurance.[9]

---

[7]National Election Studies for 1978 through 1984, conducted by the Center for Political Studies, University of Michigan, and reported in Robert A. Bernstein, *Elections, Representation, and Congressional Voting Behavior: The Myth of Constituency Control* (Englewood Cliffs, NJ: Prentice Hall, 1989), pp. 15–16.

[8]Bernstein, *Elections, Representation, and Congressional Voting Behavior,* p. 18.

[9]1988 National Election Study, analyzed in Robert S. Erikson, Norman R. Luttbeg, and Kent L. Tedin, *American Public Opinion,* 4th ed. (New York: Macmillan, 1991), p. 245.

Voters' Ignorance of Policy Issues

Even knowing a candidate's position, a voter cannot use the ballot intelligently to signal a policy preference unless he or she has such a preference. This requires some knowledge about the issue, together with enough reflection on it to form a judgment regarding what to seek or avoid.

Few issues generate this degree of knowledge and reflection. For example, after nearly a decade of national media coverage of U.S. involvement in Central America, 47 percent of those polled in the late 1980s did not know that Nicaragua is in Central America. More than half those interviewed said they "hadn't been following the controversy" or had "no opinion" as to whether the United States was supporting the current government of Nicaragua or the people fighting against the government.[10] Approximately a quarter of the electorate consistently said throughout the 1980s that they had not paid attention to the problem of establishing a homeland for Palestinians on Israeli-occupied territory, and about a fifth did not know whether they agreed or disagreed with the Palestinians.[11]

Voters do tend to cast their ballots in ways that seem intelligible in presidential contests. In 1988, of voters ranked moderately liberal (according to their policy opinions ascertained by interviewers), 69 percent chose Dukakis, while 74 percent of voters ranked moderately conservative chose Bush.[12] So it would be a mistake to think that voters are fools. But the extent of information and thoughtful policy opinion is sharply limited. As a group of public opinion scholars summarize the relation between knowledge, opinion, and voting,

> Perhaps half or more of American citizens have difficulty even understanding the conventional ideological debate between liberals and conservatives. About the same number lack understanding of basic party differences on contemporary policy issues. These individuals are often on the sidelines when the game of politics is played.[13]

Issues Not Put to Voters

Voter control also is attenuated because candidates do not take a stand on most policy issues at elections. Some concerns arise only after an election, are acted on, and die before the next election. Because elected functionaries make thousands of judgments annually, clearly politicians will not ventilate a high proportion of these for voters at election time. But even some major,

---

[10]Sobel, "Public Opinion About U.S. Intervention," pp. 114–15, 120–21.

[11]Alvin Richman, "American Attitudes Toward Israeli-Palestinian Relations in the Wake of the Uprising," *Public Opinion Quarterly* 53 (Fall 1989):415–30.

[12]Erikson et al., *American Public Opinion,* pp. 246–49.

[13]Erikson et al., *American Public Opinion,* p. 104.

enduring issues simply do not come into focus during election campaigns: The contentious and longlasting issue of civilian nuclear power rarely has been contested explicitly between competing candidates. Military nuclear wastes, the space shuttle, and the savings and loan debacle likewise have not arisen as differences between candidates in ways that voters could act on—in part, perhaps, because influential members of Congress from both parties found the issues embarrassing. Nor have policy actions pertaining to ozone depletion or the greenhouse effect been made into campaign issues. On most policy questions, then, candidates do not present citizens with a choice.

Single Dimension of the Vote

Even if all other obstacles were transcended, a fundamental feature of elections still would interfere with voter control. Consider the dilemma facing a voter who wants to make a sensible response to a candidate advocating an innovative policy. The new idea might be attractive if it is without cost to taxpayers but much less attractive if it requires substantially increased taxes. The voter needs to be able to vote yes or no depending on what new taxes will be imposed. But election campaigns ordinarily offer no realistic possibility of knowing, because funding of a new program typically occurs separately from authorization of the program; indeed, in the United States entirely different congressional committees typically dominate the two policy actions.

To use the vote effectively, a voter also would need to know whether inauguration of the candidate's new program implies termination of an old program. In other words, the voter always needs to know the implication of one choice for other choices. Before supporting an opponent of nuclear power, for example, it would be sensible to know what alternative sources of power will be used and what the candidate proposes to do about coal-burning power plants' contributions to acid rain and to the greenhouse effect.

Elections almost always proceed without specifying essential conditions or implications like these. A ballot consequently does not permit expression of more than the crudest of policy choices.

One Vote versus Many Policies

For the informed voter who knows precisely what he or she wants and what the candidates stand for, there remains another obstacle: one vote but many policy preferences. If a voter agrees with candidate Smith on fifteen issues, but agrees with candidate McNally on ten others, how can a single vote be used as an effective signal? Worse yet, what is to be done if a voter agrees with Smith on most issues but finds that McNally's few areas of agreement seem especially important? However one resolves the dilemma, it will fail to communicate anything to the winning candidate about the voter's intentions on any particular issue.

Electoral Mechanisms

Different systems of voting have significant effects on the ability of voters to translate their views into policy. In some proportional representation systems, whatever percentage of the popular vote a party gets, it is awarded that same percentage of seats in Parliament. When a new party arises, like the Greens did in many European nations in the 1980s, it is easy for even a small minority of voters to translate their views into a few voices in the legislature. It also is easy for the electorate to signal displeasure with government, since one votes for or against each party as a whole, and reductions in a party's electoral percentage are immediately translated into lost seats.

On the other hand, it is virtually impossible for voters in these systems to get rid of top elected officials within a particular party. For even in the extraordinary case of a 50 percent decline in a party's vote from one election to the next, since candidates are put onto party lists roughly in order of seniority, the effect would be to get rid of only the more junior office holders.

Does this mean that single-member districts are preferable, as in Britain and the United States, so voters can decide who wins each position? Not necessarily. Prior to the 1990 U.S. elections there was widespread disgust with Congress, especially its inability to reach agreement on a tax and budget package that would cut the deficit. Opinion polls suggested that voters were ready for a significant change. But the November elections returned to office all but one incumbent Senator and well over 90 percent of the incumbent members of the House of Representatives, and there was virtually no change in the balance of party representation in Congress. Incumbents won because of their personal popularity with constituents, gained in part by having "the overwhelming majority of staff people in any congressional office work on constituent service, not legislative research," helping expedite social security claims, promptly answering letters, blanketing the legislator's district with newsletters.[14] Under the proportional representation system, incumbents cannot win re-election in this way since they stand for election as a party bloc rather than as individuals.

Do voters therefore exercise more leverage over policy in nations that use proportional representation? There are confounding factors.[15] In multiparty systems, leaders of the larger parties may bargain away some campaign promises in order to win the support of smaller parties. Israel's Labor party, elected on a peace platform in 1992, formed a governing coalition in this way. Thus

[14]Alan Ehrenhalt, "PAC Money: Source of Evil or Scapegoat?," *Congressional Quarterly Weekly Report* (January 11, 1986):99. For details on how members of Congress cultivate their constituencies, see Richard F. Fenno, *Home Style: House Members in Their Districts* (Boston: Little Brown, 1978).

[15]An additional tradeoff is that voters may get to cast only a single ballot every three or four years in systems where voting is done nationally using proportional representation arranged by party bloc, whereas in candidate-centered systems such as the U.S. one can vote for many different offices, with some election coming around virtually every year.

continued a tradition in which that nation's leaders have "enormous leeway for flexibility in making Israel's foreign and defense policies," evading much influence by voters.[16] Cleavages among voters, the number of parties and their ideological orientation, and other factors also confound any straightforward relation between public sentiment, voting, and elected functionaries' subsequent behaviors.[17]

The intensity with which people hold their views introduces additional complexity. When a large majority of voters prefer A over B, and an election shows A winning over B, most people would say the election results make sense. But if only 51 percent of the voters mildly prefer A, while 49 percent intensely prefer policy option B, we feel less sure that A's winning make sense.

No voting system can solve such problems as these in determining an overall social choice from individuals' opinions.[18] Voters' views thus can be at least partially thwarted in various ways by many methods of voting for candidates.

HELP FROM POLITICAL PARTIES?

Political parties can help reduce some—but by no means all—of the obstacles to effective use of the vote. A strong political party is in a position to formulate a package of mutually supportive policy proposals. A voter can then weigh and choose among two or a few parties' packages rather than contend with a dozen or more candidates for various offices, each with a different program.

In many political systems, national party officials exert considerable control over the selection of candidates; elected officials whose views diverge too sharply may be refused a party's nomination at the next election. The parties thereby tie candidates to a collective platform, so a voter can predict what many of a candidate's policy positions are likely to be.[19] In Germany, for example, a voter needs merely to become familiar with the Christian Democratic Union, Social Democratic Party, and a few other parties' general positions; it is not necessary to know anything about candidates other than their party affiliation.

In the American system, the Democratic and Republican parties now

[16]Asher Arian, Ilan Talmud, and Tamar Hermann, *National Security and Public Opinion in Israel* (Boulder, CO: Westview, 1988), p. 79.

[17]See Douglas Rae, *The Political Consequences of Electoral Laws* (New Haven, CT: Yale University Press, 1967).

[18]See Kenneth Arrow, *Social Choice and Individual Values* (New York: John Wiley & Sons, Inc., 1951) for additional difficulties in inferring social from individual preferences.

[19]On the British case, see Max Beloff and Gillian Peele, *The Government of the UK: Political Authority in a Changing Society,* 2nd ed. (New York: W. W. Norton, 1985), especially pp. 222–26 and 239–41.

commit themselves only vaguely on policy, and candidates freely disavow the party platform.[20] But parties still help in making political life less fragmented, with each party having at least a vague orientation from which voters can infer some of its general policy directions. Thus, Democratic party leaders "typically display the stronger urge to elevate the low born, the uneducated, the deprived minorities, and the poor in general, . . . [while] Republican leaders subscribe in greater measure to the symbols and practices of individualism, laissez-faire, and national independence."[21] Cleavages between the parties sharpened in the 1980s as the Reagan administration put abortion and other moral issues on the political agenda, undertook the Iran-Contra arms deal, began the Star Wars missile defense system, and cut environmental protection programs.[22] Party conflicts over these and other issues enhanced the cues available to voters.

Limits on Party Effectiveness

Parties often fail to help citizens translate their votes into popular control over public policy, however. First, parties sometimes help minorities rather than majorities, putting together a winning coalition by appealing to several groups with views intense enough to bring them to the polls instead of trying to appeal to a more apathetic majority. Conversely,

> Some policy alternatives are simply ruled out because members anticipate a popular outcry or fear the retribution of organized interest groups. A vote for even a mild form of gun control seems too risky for most members of Congress, who see, or think they see, the National Rifle Association poised in the shadows.[23]

Such an approach may bring in donations and votes, but will not serve as an instrument of majorities.[24]

Parties also cannot be of much assistance in helping voters register their policy preferences if voters do not let themselves be guided by policy considerations and party cues. In the 1950s, some 70 percent of adults belonged to the

---

[20]In New York State and some other American states, party discipline actually holds legislators to a common position about as firmly as in some European systems.

[21]Herbert McClosky, Paul J. Hoffman, and Rosemary O'Hara, "Issue Conflict and Consensus Among Party Leaders and Followers," *American Political Science Review* 54 (1960):406–27, quote from p. 426.

[22]Paul Allen Beck, "Incomplete Realignment: The Reagan Legacy for Parties and Elections," pp. 145–71 in Charles O. Jones, ed., *The Reagan Legacy: Promise and Performance* (Chatham, NJ: Chatham House Publishers, 1988).

[23]William J. Keefe, *Congress and the American People,* 3rd ed. (Englewood Cliffs, NJ: Prentice Hall, 1988), p. 214.

[24]An illuminating theoretical discussion of minorities rule is in Robert A. Dahl, *A Preface to Democratic Theory* (Chicago: University of Chicago Press, 1956), chapters 4 and 5. For a critique of interest-group liberalism—the tendency to put government at the service of organized minorities—see Theodore J. Lowi, *The End of Liberalism,* 2nd ed. (New York: W. W. Norton, 1979).

same political party their two parents had, voted for the same party for each office, and continued supporting the same party at each election. Since then, an increasing percentage of the American public has come to identify with neither party—voting independently "for the best candidate."[25] Because parties provide one of the few mechanisms for aggregating and translating public sentiment into policy, turning away from them makes that task even harder. But habitual voting unrelated to a party's policy stance hardly seems superior to thoughtful independent voting. Neither approach is likely to provide the electorate with much control over policy.

A third limitation on party effectiveness is that candidates and parties often appeal to voters on grounds other than party or policy. And millions of people respond, looking at office holders and candidates on personal more than on programmatic grounds. Trust in a candidate, for example, appears to play a role in many voters' decisions; mentioned especially in surveys is whether the candidate is perceived to be "honest, sincere; keeps promises; man of integrity; means what he says; not tricky, open/candid; straight-forward; fair."[26] As two opinion researchers put it a generation ago, before television campaigning had developed to its current extent,

> There is a widespread belief in the intimacy of television, . . . [and] viewers believe they have "seen for themselves." . . . When the formats of political telecasts are adapted to this belief, they emphasize the personal qualities of a politician rather than his purely political qualifications. . . . [This suggests that] complex policy matters and public problems can be factored down to simple alternatives. The search for "truth" becomes a search for "trust."[27]

Partly because political campaign tactics have adapted to take maximal advantage of television, "candidate-orientedness has increased for everyone."[28] Who could endorse voting for untrustworthy candidates? But when trust is emphasized at the cost of policy, the electorate's substantive input into policy making suffers.

Political campaigning is criticized extensively throughout the world, but few nations feature party competition with as little substantive conflict as that in the United States.

---

[25]For an overview of changing and unchanging voting habits, see Richard G. Niemi and Herbert F. Weisberg, eds., *Controversies in Voting Behavior,* 2nd ed. (Washington, DC: Congressional Quarterly Press, 1984); and Eric Smith, *The Unchanging Voter* (Berkeley: University of California Press, 1990).

[26]Glenn R. Parker, "The Role of Constituent Trust in Congressional Elections," *Public Opinion Quarterly* 53 (Summer 1989):175–96, quote from p. 182.

[27]Kurt Lang and Gladys Engel Lang, *Politics and Television* (Chicago: Quadrangle Books, 1968), pp. 210–11.

[28]Scott Keeter, "The Illusion of Intimacy: Television and the Role of Candidate Personal Qualities in Voter Choice," *Public Opinion Quarterly* 51 (Fall 1987):344–58.

Other limitations.   Many Americans live in municipalities in which candidates for local office do not run under party labels. In other areas, one party is so dominant that competition is ineffective, so the only real competition is via primary elections within a party. Under these circumstances, party does not help voters achieve control over policy.

Party competition also fails to help put control over policy into the hands of voters when parties fail to respond effectively as new issues enter politics and voters' attitudes and wishes shift. For reasons of motivation and ideology, as well as of information and competence, mainstream parties have been slow to understand and respond to new groupings among voters. Thus, Green parties have sprung up in Germany, the Netherlands, and elsewhere because existing parties failed to appeal sufficiently to those favoring strong environmental policies. Ross Perot's outsider presidential candidacy in 1992 likewise was nourished by widespread discontent with the major parties' ideas and track records. But new views among the American electorate cannot readily be served via new parties, because it is virtually impossible for a new party to win enough seats to become established in the United States.

CONCLUSION

Elections are not completely toothless, of course. Competing candidates and parties surely do adapt toward what they perceive will be popular with voters. While this often means being responsive to organized and vocal minorities, the electoral incentive does serve majority will in at least one important way: Except for small parties appealing to specialized subgroups of the population, every party and candidate has an incentive to avoid offending clear majorities. Virtually no politician now dares speak against environmental preservation, for example, unless it can be depicted as costing jobs.

For the full import of this conclusion, imagine two parties or candidates competing to win an election. At the last moment the election is canceled and a winning party is chosen by the toss of a coin. If both parties had offered voters those policies that a clear large majority wanted, on those issues it would not matter to voters which party won the toss. The effect of the anticipated election would have been to drive both parties to nearly identical positions on each of the policies that an unmistakable majority favored.

Compared with the lofty goals supposedly served by elections, avoiding giving offense to large majorities is not much of an accomplishment. But it looks somewhat better when compared with the miserable performance of most nondemocratic systems where large majorities are routinely ignored.

Still, for all the reasons covered above, elections are relatively weak vehicles for translating citizens' needs and judgments into policy. The frequent claim by a winning candidate that he or she has a mandate from the electorate to lower taxes, to take a harder line toward unfriendly nations, or to cut federal payrolls is ordinarily fraudulent. A candidate rarely knows whether victory was due to a stand on any single issue—or in spite of the stand. And if the outcome ever could be attributed to some single issue, then on all other issues the winner would be without guidance from the electorate. When a candidate is elected without a majority of the popular vote, as was true of President Clinton in the three-way race with Bush and Perot in 1992, interpretation of the results in policy terms becomes even more difficult.

Given all the very serious limitations on the possibilities of using elections to promote intelligent, democratic policy making, why is there such widespread acceptance of elections as the linchpin of democracy? Why not more probing of alternative ways to make public policy responsive to majority wishes? One barrier to such probing, analyzed further in chapters 8 through 10, is that citizens have been taught not to question the fundamental contours of the contemporary political order. If so, they may be incapable of seriously entertaining proposals for systematic improvements in the degree of democracy now being practiced, including proposals for more direct democracy, or for other possible improvements in electoral arrangements—improvements that might bring more citizens' ideas, more effectively, into the interactive processes by which policy evolves.

Chapter 5

Elected Functionaries

Because electoral controls are too imprecise to determine more than the broadest contours of policy making, direct authority rests largely in the hands of elected functionaries, their appointees, and civil servants. This would be true even if remediable shortcomings in candidate voting systems were corrected, and even if referenda like those in Switzerland and some American states were held as often as practicable.[1]

Mass publics cannot do some of the real work of policy making, such as distilling rough ideas about social problems and opportunities into polished proposals ready for a vote, or fleshing out and adapting policies via policy implementation. There simply are too many decisions to be made, with each nation's elected functionaries developing or modifying hundreds of laws annually in addition to reaching a myriad of judgments during line-by-line budget appropriations. Cabinet ministers in the Japanese Diet and Israeli Knesset and their counterparts throughout the world not only share these responsibilities for new legislation and budgeting but also have additional tasks such as for-

---

[1]A sustained argument for the feasibility of greatly expanded direct democracy is in Christa Daryl Slaton, *Televote: Expanding Citizen Participation in the Quantum Age* (New York: Praeger, 1991). For a more skeptical appraisal of numerous experiments such as those utilizing interactive cable TV systems, see F. Christopher Arterton, *Teledemocracy: Can Technology Protect Democracy?* (Beverly Hills: Sage, 1986).

eign diplomacy and for administration of policy. So even if citizen participation were increased dramatically, as it probably should be, coping with the heavy load of demands on policy making could never be done primarily through the slow and cumbersome processes for citizen deliberation and voting.[2]

Comprising as they do a tiny fraction of the citizenry, elected functionaries constitute an elite of sorts. Essential to the possibility of democratic governance though they are, elected elites simultaneously pose a threat to the prospects for intelligent, democratic policy making. For if the political elite fails to perform, the polity as a whole will suffer—and political elites fail routinely, though different observers will perceive different degrees, types, and areas of failure. Thus, a great many observers of American politics in the Reagan-Bush era perceived "a frightening inability of the nation's leaders to face, much less define and debate, the unprecedented problems and opportunities facing the country."[3] By no means is this sort of criticism limited to American politics.

Among other causes of defaults by a political elite is the tendency to lose touch with ordinary people's problems. For example, as Washington, D.C., has become increasingly affluent in the past generation or two with the rise of big government and with the accompanying establishment in the city of permanent corporate lobbying offices with highly paid employees,

> The general political vision was inevitably warped by the gilded prosperity that politicians see all around them. The federal government is now situated in the best-educated and best-paid metropolitan area in the nation. The capital of democracy is seated in a city where citizens of average means cannot afford to live. . . . The general affluence makes it harder for the people in power to see the contradictory social facts beyond their own everyday experience.[4]

Elected and appointed functionaries working in London, Paris, and other national capitals experience something of the same phenomenon. Of course there are a great many additional reasons why political elites might have "warped political vision" and might fail to face up to a nation's problems. Some stem from the sharply limited effectiveness of elections as instruments of policy debate and judgment, already discussed; other reasons for elite default are covered in later chapters, such as those on interest groups and political in-

[2]On the prospects for enhanced citizen control, see, among many other sources, Benjamin Barber, *Strong Democracy: Participatory Politics for a New Age* (Berkeley: University of California Press, 1984); Robert A. Dahl, *A Preface to Economic Democracy* (Berkeley: University of California Press, 1985); and James S. Fishkin, *Democracy and Deliberation: New Directions for Democratic Reform* (New Haven: Yale University Press, 1991).

[3]Kevin Phillips, *The Politics of Rich and Poor: Wealth and the American Electorate in the Reagan Aftermath* (New York: Random House, 1989), p. ix.

[4]William Greider, *Who Will Tell the People: The Betrayal of American Democracy* (New York: Simon & Schuster, 1992), p. 49.

equality. First, however, this chapter analyzes difficulties for policy making arising from the complex institutional arrangements within which elected functionaries must work.

COMPLICATIONS OF DEMOCRATIC POLICY MAKING

Although the number of elected officials is very small compared with the citizenry as a whole, there is a relatively large number of influential functionaries in a democratic political system compared with most nondemocratic systems. Because hundreds of national elected officials have to cooperate with each other, certain problems arise for policy making. In particular, by constitutional design or by custom, numerous governmental arrangements come about for channeling conflict and promoting cooperation among elected functionaries.

These arrangements decrease the predictability with which any one functionary can expect his or her actions to achieve any specific intended effects. The organizational complications also increase the difficulty of assigning responsibility to any particular participants. Democratic rules, in short, turn small systems of clique or oligarchy in nations like Iraq into huge pluralistic policy-making systems difficult to understand, difficult to design for predictable outputs, and difficult to participate in effectively. The gains from democracy are bought at a cost: The sense of impotence that sometimes troubles both ordinary citizens and government officials derives partly from the complications of democracy, complications that sometimes thwart and disappoint would-be activist presidents such as Bill Clinton.

Complications of Liberty

Designers of political systems did not singularly attend to considerations of efficient and democratic policy making, because another consideration loomed even larger: curbing the power of rulers to engage in arbitrary action. Political reformers in many nations, especially the United States, wanted liberty, not popular control of policy making nor maximally efficient or effective policy making. Opponents of royal power sought to guarantee certain liberties to the nobility, aristocracy, and an emerging middle class. In addition to substantive liberties such as freedom of worship, upper and middle classes won procedural guarantees and a share of governmental authority, which could be used to protect and enhance their other liberties. Many of these libertarian arrangements create complications for policy making.

One family of complications arises out of a deliberately created division and overlapping of authority. The U.S. president and Congress play specialized roles, and interfere with each other. The president sometimes vetoes acts of Congress, and Congress sometimes turns down the president's requests for funds. The familiar term *separation of powers* refers to such specialization through division of authority, and *checks and balances* refers to mutual interference through overlapping authority.

These and other libertarian rules complicate policy making in many ways. Requiring legislation to pass through two houses rather than one, for example, means that advocates have to win two rounds whereas opponents only need to win one. Presidential and gubernatorial veto powers give opponents a third opportunity to block policy innovations; amplifying this disproportionate influence is the two-thirds rule for overriding vetoes. Altogether, these arrangements make it more difficult to carry through *any* legislative program; if it is fair to assume that government action is more likely to ameliorate social problems than is inaction, then division of authority may tend to reduce the intelligence of the policy-making process by making problem solving more difficult.

These arrangements designed to protect liberty arguably reduce the degree of democracy in policy making as well, for a political minority can block legislation desired by a majority if the minority controls even one of the three institutions whose assent is needed. The notion of majority rule is much less straightforward than usually supposed—how ought nonparticipants to be counted, for example? There are particular circumstances in which majorities perhaps ought not prevail—as when a minority's civil liberties are at stake, or when a large and intense minority confronts a lukewarm majority.[5] But there is no democratic rationale for a political system that is antimajoritarian across the board.

Other less significant libertarian rules include assignment of two senators to each state, rather than by population, thereby diluting the influence of each person in more populous states; division of authority among federal, state, and local governments; and granting formal authority for choosing a president to the Electoral College, which could have obstructed popular control over the 1992 presidential contest, in the event of a three-way deadlock due to the candidacy of Ross Perot. All these devices hark back to the intention to curb a potential overconcentration of authority in government, a laudable goal but one that conflicts with the intention to provide political arrangements enhancing the potential for intelligent, popular control over policy making.

No other Western nation fragments policy making to the extent achieved by U.S. constitutional arrangements and political customs. But France has a president elected independently of the National Assembly, Germany has two houses of its parliament, and additional nations have some elements of overlap or division of authority. Moreover, every democratic nation creates a second set of liberties that complicate policy making: protection of private property rights. This set of guarantees makes it more difficult for government to solve

[5]See Robert A. Dahl, *Democracy and Its Critics* (New Haven, CT: Yale University Press, 1989).

many social problems, in part because the affluent can use their funds as political resources to oppose policy options that would be inconvenient for them. The special forms of veto power associated with protection of property rights are discussed more fully in chapter 8 (on business), chapter 9 (on political inequality), and chapter 10 (on impaired inquiry).

ORGANIZING AND COORDINATING

Organization is crucial for coordination of work among many participants in political life, yet organization also creates problems. Democratic and intelligent policy making is both promoted and obstructed by the way the work of elected officials is organized.

In the Legislature

Any one elected functionary has to act on more issues than a single person could ever fully understand. And each needs to cooperate with more colleagues than could be engaged in sustained discussion. In one year in the House of Representatives, for example, nearly 10,000 bills and over 1,500 resolutions were introduced, each calling for at least one judgment. The 435 members cannot handle such a flow without special arrangements, and their work therefore requires organizational machinery. Even the 100-member U.S. Senate, while far less rigid than the House in its organization and operations, has elaborate arrangements for dividing and coordinating work.

The congressional committee system is part of this government within a government. With some exceptions, legislation comes to the floor of the House or Senate only after a committee has considered it and has made a positive recommendation. Only a small fraction of bills survive committee scrutiny; of those that do, fellow legislators more often than not follow committee recommendations or amend the bills only in minor ways. Although an understandable and even necessary practice, this can have disastrous results. In 1980, the Senate voted to increase federal insurance coverage of savings deposits from $40,000 to $50,000; the House did not approve any increase, so the matter had to be resolved along with many other issues by a conference committee. One high-ranking member of the House delegation, in a late-night markup session, apparently "snuck" into the complex banking bill at the behest of the banking industry a provision raising the insurance limit to $100,000 per account. The subsequent conference report sailed through the full House and Senate with essentially no debate, exposing taxpayers to many hundreds of billions of dollars in liability, and contributing to the banking failures of the 1980s.[6]

---

[6]Described in Brooks Jackson, *Honest Graft: Big Money and the American Political Process* (New York: Alfred A. Knopf, 1988). Also see R. Dan Brumbaugh, Jr., *Thrifts Under Siege: Restoring Order to American Banking* (Cambridge, MA: Ballinger, 1988).

The committees, each with a chair granted substantial authority, can be thought of as a group of semi-independent "little legislatures." Not supervised by any supercommittee nor joined together via a coordinating body such as a legislative cabinet, committees and even subcommittees practice a striking degree of autonomy. Such specialization and autonomy bring a likelihood that members of the relatively small committees, and the even smaller subcommittees, will neglect considerations that other legislators would consider important.

Thus, the Senate Armed Services Committee for decades failed to pay adequate attention to the management of radioactive wastes generated by military nuclear weapons programs. The House Science, Space and Technology Committee failed for many years to uncover deep and enduring problems at NASA, problems that led eventually to the *Challenger* space shuttle disaster in 1986. Despite widespread public concern and sustained congressional attention, the Hubble Space Telescope fiasco five years later, as well as the flip-flops on the space station design, illustrates the committee's ongoing failure to stimulate effective reorganization at NASA.[7] Such omissions and biased actions occur in part because committees develop close working relationships with the agencies and interest groups in their domain and come to take for granted practices that outsiders would question.[8]

Governmental institutions in other nations have different methods of dividing work among top policy makers, but all must do so to get even the mediocre results now achieved in coping with complex problems facing technological societies. Wherever responsibilities are delegated, however, vision will be narrowed, and the degree of intelligence and democracy may be reduced.

Legislative Parties

Political parties serve as a powerful organizing force in many political systems, especially those with a parliamentary form of government in which elected members almost always vote with the other members of their party. Compared with British parliamentary politics, American political parties shape policy only weakly in Congress. Democrats and Republicans do generally vote with others of their party when it comes to choosing committee chairs and the Speaker of the House. Likewise they bind themselves, at least loosely, together in a party caucus in each house and elect officers such as party whip and majority or minority leader. Various party committees also help achieve

[7]Arthur L. Levine et al., "The Future of the U.S. Space Program: A Public Administration Critique," *Public Administration Review* 52 (March/April 1992):183–203.

[8]On triangular access patterns among congressional committees, bureaucratic agencies, and interest groups, see Theodore Lowi, *The End of Liberalism* (New York: W. W. Norton, 1969), chapter 4.

a measure of cooperation among party members; if each member were to go his or her own way, no member could effect any policy.

Once legislators concede any significant authority to party leaders, the leaders can strengthen their control by indirect use of authority. In parliamentary systems, where members of the majority party actually become cabinet ministers and take charge of running the government, the prospect of receiving a ministerial position is sufficiently attractive that party leaders can usually hold a legislator to a party program by threatening to deny him or her a leadership role. Even in presidential systems, party leaders can win a degree of authority through their power to offer reciprocal favors. In the U.S. Congress, this means less than it used to, but party leaders still "can do a lot towards seeing whether your bill will get on the calendar," can help in "pushing hearings along," and have some discretion over committee assignments. Every legislator's admitted need for information and advice points to still another reason for following party leadership on policy: Because no legislator can be well informed on any but a small number of issues, when in doubt it often makes sense to "follow the party—and there's always something that's in doubt."[9]

Executive Leadership

Most nations' elected officials achieve coordination by practicing a high degree of deference toward the leaders of their political party. Once the prime minister and senior cabinet ministers have debated a policy problem and reached a verdict—within very broad limits, set partly by what they think their junior colleagues in the party will go along with—the actual parliamentary vote usually is close to a formality. This greatly expedites policy making, obviously, compared with the sometimes torturously slow American system. But the efficiency comes at some cost, reducing opportunities for diverse participants outside the narrow circle of the cabinet to have policy adjusted to their concerns. French governments in the 1970s and 1980s, for example, made civilian nuclear power the centerpiece of French energy policy, despite opposition from a majority of the public.[10]

Needing more leadership than its autonomous committees and weak party caucuses provide, the U.S. Congress turns to the executive for leadership and coordination, including a requirement to recommend to Congress a budget of proposed expenditures each year. Roughly 80 percent of the bills enacted into law now originate in the executive branch, with the presidents and their appointees largely determining the policy-making agenda of Congress, although less so than a British prime minister and cabinet do for Parliament.

---

[9]Quotations from legislators are from John C. Wahlke and others, *The Legislative System* (New York: John Wiley & Sons, Inc., 1962), pp. 366–67.

[10]Dorothy Nelkin and Michael Pollak, *The Atom Besieged: Extraparliamentary Dissent in France and Germany* (Cambridge, MA: MIT Press, 1981).

Democratic systems require inventive leadership for the management of conflict among the many interests free to press their demands. In particular, they require leadership capable of restructuring political controversy, finding common grounds for action among groups otherwise in contention, and moving a debate from profitless posturing toward new vision and action. That kind of leadership can spring from anywhere in the system, in principle; but the obligation and opportunities to provide it rest especially on the president or prime minister.

But will the leadership role actually be taken up? Will it be handled in ways that promote intelligent social problem solving? Will it be responsive to public needs and wishes? Despite hundreds, perhaps thousands, of studies of political leadership, there is agreement neither on the personal qualities that help a person be effective in a high-level political role, nor on the design of political institutions that will tend to select the "right" persons, nor on institutional frameworks that will enable such persons to coordinate, motivate, and otherwise "lead."[11]

Given that there is no agreed formula for choosing or empowering effective leadership, it is perhaps not surprising that political leadership so often disappoints. Indeed, given the poverty of understanding and agreement, it would be very surprising to find otherwise. One implication is that it is realistic to expect that persons inappropriate for leadership roles sometimes or often will be elevated to those roles, and that they will perform poorly. Moreover, even politicians who are in some sense appropriate for high-level positions will routinely disappoint a nontrivial fraction of the public, for many reasons including the fact that interests are in conflict so helping one cause may harm others. In addition to disappointing those partisans who lose on a given policy or set of policies, those holding key governmental roles may coordinate badly because the organizational or other obstacles are too high. Thus, coordination in the American system is a nightmare compared with the Japanese; coordination in the United States is harder even than in the Canadian system with all its difficulties around the issue of provincial autonomy. Furthermore, the loose design of electoral accountability systems (see chapter 4 on elections) means that those elected to office often will be able to get away with quite a bit of behavior that the majority of the electorate would disapprove.

The Bush administration's behavior on environmental issues was illustrative. Elected to office with a promise of being "an environmental president," President Bush instead used the latitude built into the office of the presidency to engage in numerous actions widely perceived as anti-environmental, including among others:

---

[11]For efforts toward a better understanding of political leadership, see James David Barber, *The Presidential Character: Predicting Performance in the White House,* 4th ed. (Englewood Cliffs, NJ: Prentice Hall, 1992); and James MacGregor Burns, *Leadership* (New York: Harper & Row, 1978).

1. Refused to sign the global biodiversity treaty negotiated at Rio in 1992;
2. Slowed down global action on ozone and carbon dioxide;
3. Decided to interpret the Endangered Species Act as not being applicable to the activities of American businesses operating in foreign countries;
4. Supported a Supreme Court case making it more difficult for environmental groups to bring suit against the government.[12]

Without claiming that the opposite actions were the right ones, since that is a matter of partisan dispute, it is apparent that there was a marked discrepancy between the claims advanced by President Bush and his actual behavior on environmental issues. Existing democratic systems have only very weak mechanisms for holding elected functionaries accountable in these circumstances.

SELF-SELECTED ROLES

These and other complexities of democratic government open a broad range of choice for elected functionaries. Even if their principal objective is to be reelected, they may not need to actually try to solve social problems in ways that would be favored by, or favorable to, a majority of the public.

In those European-style electoral systems where the key to reelection is staying in good stead with other party leaders, elected functionaries may well have incentives to behave in ways quite different from those necessary for running a nation well. Thus, despite growing disenchantment with Prime Minister Margaret Thatcher's policies in the late 1980s, policies widely perceived as economically and politically disastrous, the great majority of Conservative Party members of Parliament long went along with whatever the Prime Minister proposed.

For American legislators elected from single-member districts, without much help or hindrance from others of their party, the key to reelection arguably is to become so well-known and popular that challengers cannot attract funding to run a formidable campaign. This may actually be achieved better by *not* spending a lot of time and energy studying issues, forming alliances with interest groups and executive branch officials, making deals with other legislators, and otherwise shepherding legislation through the many hoops it needs to jump in order to become law. For it is very difficult to get credit with constituents for all that effort; and the time spent doing it takes away from activities that do pay direct electoral dividends.

These activities include winning benefits for one's district or state, such as employment-generating construction projects like the controversial $8 billion superconducting supercollider in Texas. Legislators can even claim credit

---

[12]*Lujan v. Defenders of Wildlife*, 1992 U.S. Lexis 3543, 60 USLW 4495, decided June 12, 1992.

for such benefits without actually doing much to win them. Assiduous cultivation of one's constituency also builds name recognition and voter loyalty, as by helping with Veteran's Administration and Social Security claims, answering letters courteously, and blanketing the district with "congressional newsletters." Another option is to take conspicuous and popular *stands* on policy issues while not actually working actively for any policy.[13]

Finally, when elected functionaries do make policy choices, they face the classic choice of options: working for policies sought (or approved) by citizens, or working for policies judged best by an elected elite.[14] The former approach is usually believed to raise the risk of unintelligent policy, the latter to reduce democratic responsiveness. As a study of foreign policy decision making puts it, most people

> want two things that often prove incompatible in practice: *democratic government* (involving ongoing competition among a range of U.S. interests and perspectives) and *effective foreign policy* (which requires settling on specific goals and pursuing them consistently).[15]

In the American system, Congress usually is associated with democratic diversity and debate, while the executive branch is considered more capable of coherent policy formation and execution. This is oversimplified, considering the frequent incoherence of executive policies such as in the Iran-Contra affair, and the equally frequent failure to develop any policy as was true of the Reagan administration regarding the savings and loan bailout, and was true of the Bush administration regarding the recession of 1990–92. Nor (as discussed in chapter 3) is coherence necessarily to be praised as much as many people think: Is it desirable to have a clear, coherent policy that turns out to be disastrously wrong—such as the Nixon Administration's decision to put multiple, independently targettable (MIRV) warheads on nuclear missiles, greatly magnifying the nuclear threat and the difficulty of achieving arms control?[16]

Each elected functionary has considerable latitude in choosing how much focus to place on foreign policy or other policy areas, what specific issues to take up, and what substantive positions to support or oppose. Sometimes this looseness in the accountability system works out well, allowing elected offi-

---

[13]These possibilities are documented and analyzed in David Mayhew, *Congress: The Electoral Connection* (New Haven, CT: Yale University Press, 1974).

[14]On the elected official's different understandings of his or her role, see Malcolm E. Jewell and Samuel C. Patterson, *The Legislative Process in the United States,* 2nd ed. (New York: Random House, 1973), pp. 407-10. For Britain, see Samuel H. Beer, *British Politics in the Collectivist Age* (New York: Alfred A. Knopf, Inc., 1966).

[15]I. M. Destler, "Executive-Congressional Conflict in Foreign Policy: Explaining It, Coping with It," in Lawrence C. Dodd and Bruce I. Oppenheimer, eds., *Congress Reconsidered,* 3rd ed. (Washington, DC: Congressional Quarterly Press, 1985), pp. 343-63, quote from p. 344.

[16]Ted Greenwood, *Making the MIRV: A Study of Defense Decision Making* (Cambridge, MA: Ballinger, 1975).

cials latitude to focus attention where they perceive opportunities to be most useful. For example, one of the legislators most knowledgeable and active in working to curb the damage done by junk bonds and other financial manipulations has been Sen. Byron Dorgan of North Dakota. "My constituents don't quite understand why I care," he says, "because we're not exposed to hostile takeovers and stuff like that in North Dakota."[17] But as a former tax commissioner with the relevant expertise, he has chosen to devote a significant portion of his attention to intricate policy matters many of his fellow legislators do not understand.

The latitude that elected functionaries have in defining their roles sometimes promotes intelligent, democratic policy and sometimes undermines it. Different observers will disagree on the proportion of each. What can be said for sure is that, with the exception of unusually salient issues (such as race relations in the American South during most of the twentieth century), by no means are elected functionaries tightly constrained to perform in particular ways. To put it differently, the system within which elected functionaries works lacks a systematic strategy for inducing them to perform in ways that lead to intelligent, democratic outcomes.

IMPLICATIONS FOR POPULAR CONTROL
AND FOR INTELLIGENT DECISION MAKING

Given all these arrangements for legislative organization and executive leadership, and given the options open to elected functionaries in how they play their roles, no straightforward relation holds between what citizens want and the policies they get. How responsive policy is to citizen needs and wishes (when citizens have judgments about such matters, and when those can be discerned) depends on the structure of the rules, authority relations, procedures, and organizations mediating between an elected official and the effect he or she exerts on policy.[18]

Since functionaries have designed political arrangements for their own convenience more than to increase the effectiveness of popular control, many aspects of legislative and executive organization actually tend to obstruct popular control. Those who design such arrangements often intend just that: to insulate themselves to some degree from the demands of the citizenry. Similarly, legislators may choose among alternative possible roles, not to enhance

---

[17]Quoted in Greider, *Who Will Tell the People?*, p. 40.

[18]Additional obstructions and convolutions could be added, such as those attending coalition governments in parliamentary systems, and those occurring when presidential systems have one party in control of the executive and a different one dominating the legislative branch, as explored in David R. Mayhew, *Divided We Govern: Party Control, Lawmaking, and Investigations, 1946–1990* (New Haven, CT: Yale University Press, 1991).

popular control but to suit their own needs. Despite longstanding complaints brought by voters and political scientists (and by some legislators as well) against congressional procedures, the internal organization of Congress continues to suit the members relatively well.[19]

Although such a state of affairs does not entirely undermine democracy, it fails to correspond closely with most democratic models of citizen control over policy making. Coupled with the weakness of elections as an instrument of popular control over policy making, one must conclude that while the rules of democracy put important powers and liberties into citizens' hands, they confer only a very loose control over policy. The intelligence of policy making, moreover, can be predicted to be highly variable insofar as it depends on the good will of elected functionaries: some will perform splendidly, others quite the opposite, and the political machinery will not systematically prefer one to the other.

[19]See Mayhew, *Congress*, pp. 81–82.

Chapter 6

Bureaucratic Policy Making

Since neither electoral processes nor the institutions within which elected functionaries work inspire great confidence in the prospects for intelligent and
democratic policy making, do civil servants and other appointed functionaries
perhaps serve as a partial corrective? Or does bureaucracy share and even
exacerbate problems found elsewhere in the policy-making process?

Bureaucracy is the largest part of any government if measured by the
number of people engaged or by the funds expended: Some 98 percent of the 3
million U.S. government employees work in the bureaucracy. Their combined
expertise obviously does bring indispensable knowledge into government:
medical researchers at the Food and Drug Administration, toxicologists at the
Environmental Protection Agency, economists at the Securities and Exchange
Commission. Bureaucrats even seem to behave more fairly than elected officials at times, as when Social Security or veterans' pensions are sent out only
to those who are legally eligible, while members of Congress sometimes seek
benefits for their constituencies irrespective of what might be equitable.[1]

[1]On the difficulties of figuring out what counts as fair or just in bureaucratic behavior, see
Jerry L. Mashaw, *Bureaucratic Justice* (New Haven, CT: Yale University Press, 1983), and Eugene
Bardach and Robert A. Kagan, *Going By the Book* (Philadelphia, PA: Temple University Press,
1982).

On the other hand, there is a widespread perception of a runaway bureaucratic machine.[2] To many taxpayers, "bureaucrats are lethargic, incompetent hacks . . . going to great lengths to avoid doing the job they were hired to do. Their agencies chiefly produce waste, fraud, abuse, and mismanagement."[3] Government bureaucracies long have had a bad reputation throughout the world: the French term *paperasserie*—"caught up in paper"—is at least a century old; and Chinese stories about unresponsive bureaucrats go back for millennia. Even though few people actually could define the term *red tape,* almost everyone knows its connotation: delay or inaction caused by excessive focus on procedure.[4] Legislators in some countries make a small industry out of intervening with government departments on behalf of constituents, sometimes taking campaign donations or outright monetary favors for doing so, as was said of the U.S. senators who became known as the Keating Five, charged with intervening with banking regulators on behalf of savings and loan millionaire Charles Keating.[5]

The general distrust of "bureaucracy" notwithstanding, citizens' interactions with government agencies actually work out fairly well much of the time. A surprisingly large number of people report coming away from bureaucratic encounters with a good opinion of government employees and with at least moderate satisfaction concerning the outcome of their transaction.[6] Journalists, social scientists, and others in positions to observe the day-to-day workings of government bureaucracies find much of their work meritorious. There is enormous variation in bureaucratic responsiveness and sensibility: Many European and Japanese bureaucracies perform admirably in certain respects, while those of some nations barely perform at all. Within each political system, some agencies are managed better than others—the U.S. Agriculture Department's food stamp program enjoys a far better reputation than the Department of Energy's (admittedly more difficult and controversial) programs for radioactive waste disposal.

What do these contradictory indications say about the degree to which

[2]For a thoughtful analysis sympathetic to this view, see Ralph P. Hummel, *The Bureaucratic Experience,* 2nd ed. (New York: St. Martin's Press, 1982), quote from p. vii.

[3]James Q. Wilson, *Bureaucracy: What Government Agencies Do and Why They Do It* (New York: Basic Books, 1989), p. x.

[4]The growth of U.S. government bureaucracy during the twentieth century provoked numerous such criticisms, including James M. Beck, *Our Wonderland of Bureaucracy* (New York: Macmillan, 1932); and Lawrence Sullivan, *Bureaucracy Runs Amuck* (Indianapolis: Bobbs-Merrill Co., 1944). For a more balanced early appraisal, see Charles S. Hyneman, *Bureaucracy in a Democracy* (New York: Harper, 1950).

[5]Morris Fiorina examines the American case of legislators making themselves indispensable to constituents in *Congress: Keystone of the Washington Establishment,* 2nd ed. (New Haven, CT: Yale University Press, 1989).

[6]See Charles T. Goodsell, *The Case for Bureaucracy,* 2nd ed. (Chatham, NJ: Chatham House Publishers, 1985), for a thoughtful case that bureaucracy works fairly well, including summaries of relevant opinion surveys.

bureaucratic policy making makes a defensibly intelligent and democratic contribution to political life? Why is the enormous collective expertise in the bureaucracy brought to bear less effectively on social problem solving than many people would want? What keeps government bureaucracies from being more responsive to popular needs and judgments?[7]

ARE BUREAUCRATS POLICY MAKERS?

Do political "leaders" set policy, and then administrators implement it? This was once the prevailing theory of government. If civil servants typically act just as messengers, merely carrying out the dictates of elected functionaries, then they could not make policy making much more intelligent or democratic. In fact, however, bureaucrats are active participants in the policy-making process: Administrative actions typically modify or set policy in the process of trying to implement it, and agencies not infrequently are instructed by elected functionaries to make policy.[8]

Indeed, if it were possible to count all the policy-making acts in any political system—choices made, attempts at persuasion, agreements reached, threats and promises made, authoritative commands given or received—one would find that, so defined, policy making rests overwhelmingly in the hands of the bureaucracy, leaving relatively few policies to be determined elsewhere.[9] Although the executive, legislature, and judiciary dominate in setting some of the most important policies, the bureaucracy predominates over a larger number, including some of the highest importance. Often "the latitude of those charged with carrying out policy is so substantial that . . . policy is effectively 'made' by the people who implement it."[10]

To understand why this must be so, consider a very simple kind of policy, a state's highway speed limit. After the legislature and governor pass a law

---

[7]This chapter deals only with bureaucratic policy making. For a larger perspective on the overall role of bureaucracy, see Peter M. Blau and Marshall W. Meyer, *Bureaucracy in Modern Society,* 3rd ed. (New York: McGraw Hill, 1987); Bruno Rizzi, *The Bureaucratization of the World* (New York: The Free Press, 1985).

[8]In an early challenge to the simplistic idea of bureaucracies as mere implementers of decisions made by elected officials, Friedrich noted that public policy "is a continuous process, the formulation of which is inseparable from its execution," in Carl J. Friedrich, "Public Policy and the Nature of Administrative Responsibility," in C. J. Friedrich and Edward Mason, eds., *Public Policy 1940* (Cambridge, MA: Harvard University Press, 1940), p. 6.

[9]Overviews of bureaucratic politics are to be found in Francis E. Rourke, *Bureaucracy, Politics, and Public Policy,* 3rd ed. (Boston: Little Brown, 1984); Guy Benveniste, *Bureaucracy,* 3rd ed. (Chatham, NJ: Chatham House Publishers), 1989; and B. Guy Peters, *The Politics of Bureaucracy,* 3rd ed. (New York: Longman, 1989).

[10]Michael Lipsky, "Standing the Study of Public Policy Implementation on its Head," in Walter Dean Burnham and Martha W. Weinberg, eds., *American Politics and Public Policy* (Cambridge, MA: MIT Press, 1978), p. 397.

setting the limit at fifty-five miles per hour, the police commissioner must determine whether to allow motorists a five or ten miles-per-hour leeway; whether to concentrate enforcement on the state's main highways or on the more dangerous two-lane secondary highways; and whether to focus on a few violators or draw officers from other tasks to issue a large number of tickets. Each patrol officer subsequently must decide how closely to follow the commissioner's instructions.

In actual practice, then, the state's operative policy may be to stop a small proportion of those driving over seventy miles per hour. A fuller understanding of the policy would have to take account of how judges handle specific cases, including whether heavier fines are levied on disreputable-looking drivers. Some people might say that only the legislature's and governor's declaration should be considered the state's policy; all else is practice rather than policy. If the aim is to understand how governments come to do what they do, however, the term *policy* needs to be applied to actual practice, not merely to formally announced intentions.

Enforcement of speed limits tends to be highly selective in part because police departments are given inadequate funds to fully implement announced policy. The same holds true for environmental laws and for many other public policies.[11] Elected officials frequently authorize programs without providing necessary funds: Legislators may miscalculate requirements or vacillate on commitment to a policy; or they may seek credit from some voters for authorizing the program and from other voters for minimizing appropriations. Especially in parliamentary systems, shifting electoral fortunes may switch policy control to a different political party with different priorities. The U.S. "Congress regularly only provides a fraction of the resources required to accomplish the regulatory tasks (it has) delegated to regulatory agencies."[12] Administrators thus are forced to allocate limited funds and staff, thereby deciding how energetically each part of a policy will be pursued.

Elected functionaries know they cannot write a law that covers all possible cases, moreover, and many legislative acts and executive orders actually are designed to require administrators to formulate policy specifics. Thus, Congress instructed the Federal Communications Commission to license television stations for "public convenience and necessity," because legislators did not want to take on the job of deciding many important aspects of licensing policy. Similarly, the law regulating interstate commerce merely forbids "unfair or deceptive acts," leaving the crucial definitions up to the Interstate Commerce Commission and to the courts.

---

[11]Walter A. Rosenbaum, *Environmental Politics and Policy,* 2nd ed. (Washington, DC: Congressional Quarterly Press, 1991).

[12]Gary Bryner, *Bureaucratic Discretion: Law and Policy in Federal Regulatory Agencies* (New York: Pergamon, 1987), p. 1.

Administrative discretion arises for additional reasons. Legislative haste may lead to imprecise or ambiguous language, requiring interpretation. Elected functionaries may be unable to agree on specifics. Or vague language may be adopted as a deliberate strategy to facilitate compromise, allowing all sides of a dispute to retain the hope that their interpretations will be embraced during the implementation process. The result is that "acts of Congress are notorious for their imprecision. Often, in fact, Congress does not determine what it wants until it sees what it gets."[13] This state of affairs obviously creates the potential for administrators to counteract the intentions of elected officials. Thus, if federal legislation designed to finance expanded child-health programs fails to specify which programs are eligible, state administrators can use the funds as they see fit, perhaps applying the new federal dollars to support existing activities and largely negating the professed policy of expanding health care.

Delegation of policy making to administrators also occurs accidentally when "the legislative process itself is so stormy and full of crosscurrents that the statute passed incorporates a number of contradictory policy guidelines, and the agency has to use its own judgment to make sense out of the mishmash."[14] Conflicting criteria may also be deliberately imposed, as when an Israeli agency charged with safeguarding workers' health also is required to take into account each industry's ability to pay. Although improved health and low cost both are reasonable goals, the first often calls for tighter workplace standards while the second calls for laxer standards. Elected functionaries may or may not realize that reconciliation of the conflict, thus a significant part of the actual determination of policy, is left in the hands of the bureaucracy.

In difficult program areas, like improving the education of disadvantaged children or reducing teenage pregnancy, legislators will often feel compelled to inaugurate programs beyond anyone's competence. Faced with the impossibility of announced policy, administrators to some degree then set their own policy. Directed by law to curb drug abuse, for example, and not really knowing how to do it, bureaucrats have experimented with a variety of policies of their own design or have simply not acted.

For all these and other reasons, appointed officials cannot merely "implement" laws and other directives from elected functionaries; instead, civil servants are compelled to participate in the policy-making process.[15]

---

[13]James W. Fesler and Donald F. Kettl, *The Politics of the Administrative Process* (Chatham, NJ: Chatham House Publishers, 1991), p. 272.

[14]Fesler and Kettl, *Politics of the Administrative Process,* p. 14.

[15]Nor is this truth confined to democratic political systems, as indicated by recent Chinese experience, discussed in Kenneth G. Lieberthal and David M. Lampton, eds., *Bureaucracy, Politics, and Decision Making in Post-Mao China* (Berkeley: University of California Press, 1992).

BUREAUCRATIC INTELLIGENCE?

Administrators indeed *are* policy makers, then. One reason it sometimes makes good sense to delegate policy-making authority to the bureaucracy is that new policies may be developed early in the life cycle of a social problem, when there is little experience on which to base a regulatory effort. It can be obvious that something needs to be done long before anyone knows enough to judge exactly what. Delegating authority to administrators often is more intelligent than making a difficult-to-reverse stab in the dark—or not acting at all. A similar rationale applies when circumstances are changing too rapidly for elected functionaries to sensibly specify regulatory requirements, as is perhaps now the case for regulation of biotechnology or telecommunications.

As the subjects of public policy have become increasingly technical over the past century, delegation of authority to experts has become the norm. Economists and bankers with the Deutches Bundesbank and Federal Reserve Board, not German or American politicians, set interest rates. Nuclear regulatory agencies staffed by radiation physicists and nuclear engineers establish criteria for the construction, operation, and maintenance of electricity-generating nuclear reactors; this is true not only in authoritarian Brazil and hierarchical-democratic Japan, but even in the more open democracies of Canada and Sweden. And while elected functionaries certainly participate influentially in environmental policy setting—as witnessed by the Bush administration's refusal to sign the Rio biodiversity treaty in 1992—still, Environmental Protection Agency bureaucrats and consultants with scientific expertise are the ones who negotiate the details of environmental regulations, such as those on formaldehyde and other chemicals suspected of causing cancer.[16] Experts surely enjoy too much deference in some policy areas, deference that tends to exclude other valid concerns and insights, such as those of residents near a Love Canal or a Three Mile Island. Still, not many of us would prefer to have elected functionaries or untrained citizens entirely take over technically laden policy tasks. So some delegation of authority to those with requisite expertise often can be applauded as eminently reasonable.[17]

Even in more traditional policy arenas, policy making often proceeds through trial and error, and the street-level bureaucrats who work with a program every day are in a much better position to observe feedback and perceive

---

[16]Sheila Jasanoff, *The Fifth Branch: Science Advisers as Policymakers* (Cambridge: Harvard University Press, 1990); Mark E. Rushefsky, *Making Cancer Policy* (Albany, NY: SUNY Press, 1986).

[17]On the interaction of expertise and political process, see David Dickson, *The New Politics of Science* (Chicago: University of Chicago Press, 1988); Joseph G. Morone and Edward J. Woodhouse, *The Demise of Nuclear Energy?: Lessons for Democratic Control of Technology* (New Haven, CT: Yale University Press, 1989); and David Collingridge, *The Management of Scale: Big Organizations, Big Decisions, Big Mistakes* (London and New York: Routledge, 1992).

what is not working than are elected officials far removed from the scene.[18] Information generated in the process of implementing programs constantly pushes policy in new directions, and administrators rather than top officials are the primary implementers, monitors, and interpreters of the trials, errors and error corrections. By their close day-by-day contact with unfolding problems and programs, bureaucrats potentially can develop a real feel for what is working, what is not, and what revised policy trials might be most worth trying.

More generally, bureaucrats' expertise can bring to bear a different problem-solving perspective, sometimes extending the frequently short-term perspectives of politicians with eyes on the next election, and perhaps counterbalancing political campaigners' tendency to throw symbol-laden verbiage at problems in lieu of effective action.[19] If enough different agencies become involved in negotiating a policy-making action, moreover, this can broaden the diversity of views considered, thereby helping to bring actual problem solving somewhat closer to the ideals sketched in chapter 3 regarding the potential intelligence of democracy.

Limitations on Bureaucratic Intelligence

The other, darker side to the story is that bureaucratic policy making also can *reduce* the intelligence of policy making. It does so when administrators

- Focus on protection of their own budgets, power, or policy turf;
- Fall into preoccupation with process instead of results; and
- Become captured to an indefensible extent by one narrow set of interests, and fail to attend to considerations necessary for sensible action within their realm of responsibility.

Personal ambition may be placed ahead of achieving a program's goals; bureaucrats may self-protectively cover up errors instead of correcting them; procedural rigidity may be used as a means of escaping responsibility, even if it means willful persistence in actions that are not succeeding, or that clearly are not worth the expense. All lead to marked deterioration in bureaucratic intelligence.

To understand why government agencies too often behave in these ways, one must begin by acknowledging the difficult circumstances under which many bureaucrats work. The stated goals of so-called criminal justice policy call for fair and speedy punishment for those who commit criminal offenses,

---

[18]Robert K. Yin and Douglas Yates, *Street-Level Governments* (Lexington, MA: Lexington Books, 1975); Michael Lipsky, *Street-Level Bureaucracy* (New York: Russell Sage Foundation, 1980).

[19]On position taking as a substitute for real action by members of Congress, see David R. Mayhew, *Congress: The Electoral Connection* (New Haven, CT: Yale University Press, 1974). More generally, see Murray Edelman, *Constructing the Political Spectacle* (Chicago: University of Chicago Press, 1988).

together with safe imprisonment and rehabilitation. The reality, however, is that police forces have inadequate resources to mount a serious effort at solving more than a fraction of reported crimes; facing overwhelming case loads and overcrowded courts, prosecutors arrange plea bargains and otherwise fail to achieve what outsiders would think of as justice; corrections officials, confronting large numbers of potentially dangerous prisoners, focus on *control* more than on rehabilitation.[20]

Higher-level administrators and bureaucrats in other areas of government do not face the same constraints as do the public employees in criminal justice, of course; but many government agencies "encounter situational factors so powerful as to make formal organizational goals all but meaningless."[21] Seen from the outside, the resulting actions often appear to be senseless—which, in terms of social problem solving, they may indeed be. But bureaucratic adaptations typically do make some sense to those within an organization.

For example, despite the fact that the Occupational Safety and Health Administration (OSHA) was formed largely because of concerns that thousands of workers could become ill from exposure to toxic chemicals, OSHA actually has focused mostly on safety rather than on chronic health problems. This seems especially strange since businesses already have considerable incentive to reduce safety hazards, because of liability claims; workers also can make a fairly direct connection between safety hazards and immediate personal harm. Chronic health problems, in contrast, may arise imperceptibly over a period of a decade or more, caused by chemical substances whose dangers cannot be detected by ordinary human senses. Yet the bias toward safety makes sense to those within the agency: It is difficult to prove that small doses of a chemical cause chronic disease; nor can bureaucrats readily specify what level of the chemical in the air would be "healthy enough." By contrast, it is comparatively easy to write regulations pertaining to safety. Wanting to avoid responsibility for making controversial judgments about highly uncertain health issues, OSHA bureaucrats have focused on safety despite a torrent of criticism regarding their misplaced priorities.[22]

The military likewise adapts tasks to fit available skills and technology, instead of vice versa. Equipped and trained to fight large-scale wars on the open terrain of Europe, the U.S. Army persisted in that approach in Vietnam, instead of adapting to fight a guerrilla war in the jungles of Southeast Asia.[23]

[20]John J. DiIulio, Jr., *Governing Prisons* (New York: The Free Press, 1987).

[21]Wilson, *Bureaucracy*, p. 38.

[22]David P. McCaffrey, *OSHA and the Politics of Health Regulation* (New York: Plenum Press, 1982).

[23]Martin van Crevold, *Command and War* (Cambridge, MA: Harvard University Press, 1985); Andrew F. Krepinevich, Jr., *The Army in Vietnam* (Baltimore, MD: Johns Hopkins University Press, 1986).

More recently, in no small part due to the armed services attempting to hold onto budgets and core missions, Soviet and American troops have remained in Germany despite the end of the Cold War, and the United States still pursues Star Wars military R&D instead of transferring scarce funds to badly needed civilian programs.[24] Of course, elected functionaries also have contributed to these choices.

SPECIALIZATION AND COORDINATION

Many of the other limitations on the intelligence of bureaucratic policy making can be traced to a single source: the necessity for creating specialized agencies for specific jobs—launching space satellites, regulating airlines, organizing diplomatic relations with other nations. Not only are there dozens or hundreds of specialized organizations in each nation's government—and more at the subnational level—but each organization further divides into bureaus, program offices, and even smaller subdivisions. Bureaucrats thereby can develop sufficient expertise and focus to have at least a chance of performing their complex tasks.

However essential, specialization and division of labor also create serious problems. For, by definition, agencies charged with one task will ignore or underemphasize other concerns. Assigned the task of building highways, for example, state highway departments often do so with little regard for other interests and values. They can pretty much go their own way, because they are excellently financed by state gasoline taxes and enthusiastically supported by construction contractors, cement manufacturers, construction workers' unions, and others who profit from large highway expenditures. Local administrators with different responsibilities—such as for urban development, recreational areas, or zoning—consequently find highway departments difficult to deal with, as do state and federal governments.

How to design the division of labor is a thorny issue, in part because any way of doing it will serve some interests better than others. In considering the Occupational Safety and Health Act, some legislators wanted key powers of enforcement given to the Department of Labor on the supposition it would sympathize with labor. Others wanted to keep those powers out of the department for the same reason. The resulting compromise granted authority to the Department of Labor to set and enforce standards, while appeals go to an independent commission, and policy innovation is partly conducted by a third agency responsible for research on occupational health standards.

[24]On bureaucrats' incentives more generally, see Andre Blais and Stephane Dion, eds., *The Budget-Maximizing Bureaucrat: Appraisals and Evidence* (Pittsburgh, PA: University of Pittsburgh Press, 1991); and Patrick Dunleavy, *Democracy, Bureaucracy, and Public Choice: Economic Explanations in Political Science* (Englewood Cliffs, NJ: Prentice Hall, 1992).

Opinions differ about when division of labor goes too far and becomes "fragmentation." A recurrent theme in twentieth century political commentary has been to call for greater planning to coordinate the many different bureaucratic units responsible for aspects of policy on urban problems, science and technology, and numerous other issues. As one political scientist puts it, "It is hard to see how policies to deal with such collective national problems can be effectively developed in a setting of widespread segmentation."[25]

The magnitude of the government's efforts does indeed pose staggering problems of resolving conflict among officials and of arranging their cooperation. Diverse agencies have overlapping responsibilities, creating the possibility of creative sharing of the overall policy burden, but also the possibility of mutual obstruction. Some nine different departments and twenty independent agencies participate in U.S. educational policy, for example, regulating roughly 15,000 local school districts; state education departments not infrequently negate or ignore the U.S. Office of Education's policy-making efforts, and vice versa. Likewise, the federal government may undertake an urban renewal project in cities, but local fire commissioners, city planners, building inspectors, courts, and other elected and appointed functionaries control what can be rehabilitated, demolished, and reconstructed. Each can make the others' policies impossible, and no policy except continuing the status quo can be established without cooperation among them.

Centralized Coordination versus Mutual Adjustment[26]

Some considerable need for coordination seems apparent. The conventional way of doing it is to put all the activities in need of coordinating under one higher authority. Thus, in response to the Arab Oil embargoes of the 1970s, the Carter administration created a Department of Energy, intended to integrate the many energy-related activities of the U.S. federal government.

Centralized coordination often disappoints, however, because its goals are unrealistic. For such coordination to work effectively, it would be necessary for the coordinators to be able to understand the relationships among all the activities to be coordinated; to formulate reasoned criteria or guidelines, according to which the coordinating will be done; and to apply those criteria in a relatively consistent way. As explained in chapter 2 on the limits of analysis, none of this is feasible.

It is impossible to unambiguously calculate even how a single complex

---

[25]Douglas Yates, *Bureaucratic Democracy: The Search for Democracy and Efficiency in American Government* (Cambridge, MA: Harvard University Press, 1982), p. 119.

[26]For a systematic comparison between centralized coordination and decentralized mutual adjustment, see Charles E. Lindblom, *The Intelligence of Democracy: Decision Making Through Mutual Adjustment* (New York: The Free Press, 1965).

policy will interact with another, much less how it will interact with all others. Nor does anyone really ever attempt such a task. The Secretary of Energy does not even have time to *read* all of the regulations and policy statements developed by the thousands of employees in the department. Nor could an administrator master the complexities of forefront research on fusion reactors, magnetohydrodynamics, X-ray lasers, and gallium arsenide solar cells, even if time were not a constraint. Nor has anyone the competence to prove, for example, whether an extra $100 million expended for research on battery-powered automobiles would do more for clean air than would an equivalent sum spent for research on coal desulfurization. Nor is it possible to come up with guidelines demonstrably superior to others for coordinating, since each guideline will give greater priority to some concerns than to others: who could say, as a general rule, how tradeoffs should be made between the two goals of increasing energy efficiency and reducing pollution?

The hope for reasoned, centralized coordination also founders because hierarchical administrative arrangements introduce additional layers of bureaucracy, exacerbating communication problems and rigidities already existing in the smaller organizations whose activities supposedly were going to be coordinated by the new, larger organization. Given these systematic and unavoidable problems, it is not surprising that few observers think the Department of Energy has done a good job with U.S. energy policy. While there is no single definition of what counts as a success or a failure in coordination, many people would be upset to learn that DOE has continued to spend $1.5 billion annually for research on civilian nuclear energy, while cutting back substantially on solar energy research. Many also would question whether "coordinated" energy policy really requires having special authorization from an Assistant Secretary every time one of the Energy Department's employees wants to ship a package by overnight express instead of using conventional mail!

So attempts at centralized coordination typically degenerate and prove disappointing. Yet clearly it would be desirable to meld together a wider range of expertise and concerns into some policy judgments than can be expected when participation is restricted to bureaucrats within a single office. Is there some other way to achieve coordination among bureaucratic units other than via centralized hierarchy? Indeed there is.

The keys to it are the same as those for sensible politics more generally: decentralized coordination via partisan interaction and mutual adjustment. When bureaucrats from different programs and agencies have to come into agreement with each other, they will to some considerable extent be led to take account of a great many more angles on a problem than if left to administer their own narrow policy segment by themselves.

The key to a potential bureaucratic intelligence of democracy lies in whether the division of labor is set up in such a way that bureaucrats have a need to adjust toward each other and toward other political participants. The more that bureaucrats reach out to adjust toward each other, the livelier can be the competition of ideas bearing on problem definition, agenda setting, option specification, and final judgement. This did not occur in management of military radioactive wastes, because a single federal agency had exclusive authority over military nuclear matters and did not have to share information or responsibility with state or federal environmental authorities. Government financial management, in contrast, is divided between the Treasury and the Federal Reserve; even though neither has formal authority to intervene in the other's affairs, by the nature of the task each is induced to take ongoing account of the other organization's ideas and actions.

When such decentralized and interactive adjustment predominates as a means of coordinating among bureaucratic units, no formal action by any one agency can be said to establish policy. Instead, policy evolves through complex and reciprocal relations among all the bureaucrats, elected functionaries, representatives of interest groups, and other participants. The outcome may be unpredictable, not fully intended by any one of the individuals who participated. It nevertheless may be a great deal more intelligent and even more democratic than normally is achieved through hierarchical coordination efforts, in the sense that a greater diversity of considerations often are brought to bear, and in the sense that no one set of participants can readily dominate others. Given all the obstacles facing centralized coordination, a high percentage of the effective coordination done in any government bureaucracy actually is achieved through decentralized mutual adjustment. That is not to say that *sufficient* coordination thereby is achieved.

DEMOCRATIC SUPERVISION OF THE BUREAUCRACY

Elected functionaries expend great effort to learn what the bureaucratic agencies are doing, and trying to induce the agencies to behave as they desire. The General Accounting office, for example, conducts audits and program reviews for Congress, publishing some 1,000 reports annually; these range from studies questioning Defense Department estimates of the effectiveness of the Stealth fighter in the Gulf War, to critiques of the EPA's progress in implementing the Clean Air Act. More than 100 subcommittees in each house of Congress hold many days of hearings annually, most of which include testimony from executive branch officials.

Such supervision or "oversight" efforts surely do succeed, to a degree.[27] Nevertheless, congressional and presidential interactions with the bureaucracy

---

[27]Joel D. Aberbach defines oversight broadly to include "congressional review of the actions of federal departments, agencies, and commissions, and of the programs and policies they administer," in *Keeping a Watchful Eye: The Politics of Congressional Oversight* (Washington, DC: Brookings, 1990), pp. 2, 217–19.

are generally held to be "unsystematic, sporadic, erratic, haphazard, ad hoc, and on a crisis basis."[28] Why is this so? Why not more supervision, and more effectiveness at it?

One reason is that the vast scope of governmental activity compared with the relatively limited time elected officials can devote to review and supervision, means that only a fraction of bureaucratic activities could be scrutinized even if every elected functionary ignored all other duties and devoted full time to it. Overwhelmed by the magnitude of the task, under these circumstances, it is not absurd to set priorities by waiting until evidence of fraud arises or until other complaints accumulate, which is all that supervision amounts to in most cases. This "fire-alarm" method has the great virtue of conserving on scarce time and attention, since it would be impossible for a few hundred national elected officials, even with the aid of their staffs, to monitor everything being done by hundreds or thousands of times that number of government bureaucrats.[29] But the inevitable result is that thousands of government programs are poorly monitored.

Other reasons for the weakness of oversight have more to do with partisan politics. Because politicians are moved by incentives to devote their efforts to activities that will help with their reelection or that will bring greater status, most will limit the number of hours spent in probes that do not promote these self-serving purposes. Although the 1976 Toxic Substances Control Act required that significant new uses of existing chemicals be approved by EPA, for example, the agency has failed to implement the requirement; despite urging by the Audubon Society, none of the environmental subcommittees in Congress has displayed interest in EPA's failure, in part because the topic is an esoteric one unlikely to win much attention from the media.

Partisanship intervenes in another sense when "some legislative committees (and subcommittees) are so amiably disposed toward 'their' agencies and programs that they are not eager to initiate penetrating inquiries into possible administrative mismanagement and program ineffectiveness."[30] This protectiveness is counteracted, to a degree, when numerous committees share responsibility for overseeing a policy area. And if multiple, conflicting interest groups are actively concerned about a government program, one may be able to prod a committee to action even if another seeks to keep the lid on.

Supervision of the bureaucracy also is hampered by the internal organization of the institutions within which elected functionaries work. In parliamentary systems, the legislative branch is weak and cabinet ministers may hesitate to question each other closely except about issues with direct bearing on the party platform or on several ministers' areas of responsibility. In the American system, appropria-

[28]Fesler and Kettl, *Politics of the Administrative Process*, p. 272.
[29]Mathew D. McCubbins and Thomas Schwartz, "Congressional Oversight Overlooked: Police Patrols versus Fire Alarms," *American Journal of Political Science* 28 (Fall 1984):165–79.
[30]Fesler and Kettl, *Politics of the Administrative Process*, p. 275.

tions committees have excellent knowledge of agency programs, together with the control over budget that could induce bureaucrats to perform as Congress desires; but they operate under stringent deadlines and have so many items to consider that their scrutiny of agency performance is not very deep.[31] The authorizing committees, those concerned more with substantive problem solving and less with budget, tend to concentrate on passage of new laws rather than on monitoring and improving the administration of existing programs.

The *quality* of supervision varies enormously among nations, and among policy areas. In the United States, members of Congress tend to engage in micromanagement of the details of agency behavior when their pet programs or constituencies are directly threatened. This makes good partisan political sense for individual legislators, but does little to promote overall effective government. Instead, arguably "Congress ought to direct more of its attention to the beginning of the rule-making process—as it writes statutes, and as agencies set priorities and establish their regulatory agendas."[32] But such recommendations, however sensible for effective policy making, stir little interest on Capitol Hill. For "congressional concern for overall policy efficiency ranges from dim to nonexistent."[33] Standing in sharp contrast is the second house of the German parliament, the Bundesrat, explicitly charged with authority over policy implementation and regarded as doing a good job of it.[34]

Even when elected functionaries become aware of serious bureaucratic errors or misdeeds, it may not be easy to correct the problem. In principle, delegated authority can always be taken away and given to another agency if bureaucrats sufficiently displease elected officials, but that is such a blunt instrument that it is rarely used. And cutting budgets is almost as difficult, since to do so is to punish the clientele of a program more than the administrators in charge of it.

Democratic versus Intelligent?

It is not always unfortunate that bureaucrats escape effective scrutiny by elected functionaries, because too much control can actually interfere with a bureaucrat's ability to perform the job.[35] Politically elected and appointed state and local school boards, for example, may be *too* effective in tying the

---

[31]Christopher H. Foreman, Jr., *Signals from the Hill: Congressional Oversight and the Challenge of Social Regulation* (New Haven, CT: Yale University Press, 1988).

[32]Bryner, *Bureaucratic Discretion*, p. 216. On the desirability of better guidance for the bureaucracy generally, see Theodore Lowi, *The End of Liberalism*, 2nd ed. (New York: W. W. Norton, 1979).

[33]Foreman, *Signals from the Hill*, p. 189.

[34]A broad cross-national comparison is made by Joel D. Aberbach, Robert D. Putnam, and Bert A. Rockman, *Bureaucrats and Politicians in Western Democracies* (Cambridge, MA: Harvard University Press, 1981).

[35]On the dangers of overmanagement, see Martin Landau and Russell Stout, Jr., "To Manage is Not to Control: Or the Folly of Type II Errors," *Public Administration Review* 39 (1979):148–56; and Guy Benveniste, *Bureaucracy*, 3rd ed. (Chatham, NJ: Chatham House Publishers, 1989).

hands of school teachers and parents; creative education, including local innovation, becomes very difficult in the face of centrally mandated curricula, texts, and other regulations.[36] Even public spirited citizen interventions can misfire: In 1983 the Ralph Nader organization called Public Citizen sued to require OSHA to adopt a tough new standard on ethylene oxide, a suspected carcinogen; to accommodate the judge's order for quick action, OSHA diverted attention away from a new asbestos standard that would have affected many more people.[37]

More generally, democratically imposed constraints may serve some goals at high expense to others. Thus, the legislated opportunity for aggrieved parties to sue federal agencies in court obviously helps protect certain rights; but if EPA administrators know that their decisions are sure to be challenged as too strict, too lenient, or both, they will spend inordinate amounts of time proving that they have solicited all possible views and reviewed every bit of evidence, documenting how and why they have decided a certain way. Given scarce time and funding, this means that the EPA spends far less time than it otherwise could actually solving environmental problems.[38]

While externally imposed constraints obviously are appropriate in a democratic political system, they do create nontrivial risks of interfering with effective problem solving. One reason is that bureaucrats tend to pay far more attention to constraints than to goals; so there is a tendency for bureaucrats to lose sight of actually trying to achieve what the organization is supposed to be doing. Bureaucrats behave in this way partly because interest groups, politicians, and administrative superiors can find out fairly easily if constraints are violated. In contrast, there are myriad ways to escape being punished for not achieving goals: They often are ambiguous or vague from the outset, are hard to measure, and factors not under the bureaucrat's control can always be found to have intervened to thwart the endeavor. Elected functionaries, however, tend to pay keen attention to development and imposition of constraints and relatively little attention to goals.[39]

CONCLUSION

In sum, delegation of authority to bureaucratic agencies is both inevitable and desirable, because elected functionaries lack time, expertise, and closeness to particular cases sufficient to shape governmental actions with the precision

[36]On the difficulties of control in education, among other policy sectors, see Judith Gruber, *Controlling Bureaucracies: Dilemmas in Democratic Governance* (Berkeley: University of California Press, 1987).

[37]*Public Citizen Research Group v. Auchter,* 554 F. Supp. 242, 1983, discussed in Jeremy Rabkin, *Judicial Compulsions: How Public Law Distorts Public Policy* (New York: Basic Books, 1989).

[38]Michael Kraft and Norman Vig, eds., *Environmental Policy in the 1990s* (Washington, DC: Congressional Quarterly Press, 1992); and Walter A. Rosenbaum, *Environmental Politics and Policy,* 2nd ed. (Washington, DC: Congressional Quarterly Press, 1991).

[39]Wilson, *Bureaucracy,* pp. 331–32.

necessary for intelligent policy. On the other hand, as policy turf is taken over by lower and lower levels within an agency, it becomes very difficult to *assure* either the good sense or the democratic responsiveness of the resulting actions.

Many of those who study bureaucracy become somewhat fatalistic about the prospects for significant reform. As one scholar puts it after a lifetime of study, public management "is a world of settled institutions designed to allow imperfect people to use flawed procedures to cope with insoluble problems."[40] Bureaucrats tend to become increasingly attuned to the imperatives of protecting their budgets, and, more generally, to what makes sense within their immediate context—rather than broader considerations. That might be fine if what one agency neglected were systematically attended to by another agency. But while democratic systems do better at that than authoritarian systems do, if the responsible agency (and associated committees and interest groups) defaults, then there will be many cases where no other agency has the legal mandate or political muscle to take over the problem solving. Thus, for many years the Federal Communications Commission failed to protect cable TV subscribers from excessive rate increases, and no other agency picked up the task.

In other words, bureaucratic organization is in some ways a necessary evil. It allows complex governments to function but sets sharp limits on the degree of intelligence and public responsiveness that ordinarily can be expected. While it does not make much sense to attack bureaucracy wholesale as political campaigners sometimes do, nor is it reasonable to expect to purge bureaucratic politics of inertia, segmentation, turf protection, and other factors limiting the intelligence and responsiveness of bureaucratic actions. The perniciousness of these factors will vary substantially, however, depending on the extent to which governmental programs become captive to narrow sets of interests and ideas.

[40]Wilson, *Bureaucracy*, p. 375.

Chapter 7

Interest Groups in Policy Making

When survey researchers ask people what they consider the main deficiency in American government, nearly half say that organized interests and lobbies obstruct democracy by exerting too much influence; more than 80 percent agree that "special interests get more from government than the people do."[1] The bad reputation of interest groups is due partly to the fact that "Americans have an enduring mistrust of the mix of politics and money."[2] In one of the most colorful depictions of interest-group politics, a *Wall Street Journal* editorial compared Washington, D.C., to "The mutants' saloon in 'Star Wars'— a place where politicians, PACs, lawyers, and lobbyists for unions, business or you-name-it shake each other down full time for political money and political support."[3]

Certainly policy making engages interest groups of extraordinary variety,

[1]ABC News/Louis Harris and Associates Poll of May 1980, quoted in Amitai Etzioni, "Making Interest Groups Work for the Public," *Public Opinion* (August/September 1982):53.

[2]Larry Sabato, "Real and Imagined Corruption in Campaign Financing," pp. 155–79 in A. James Reichley, ed., *Elections American Style* (Washington, DC: Brookings, 1987), quote from p. 178.

[3]"Cleaning Up Reform," *Wall Street Journal* (November 10, 1983):3, quoted in Sabato, 1987, p. 178.

especially in the United States. These include the National Rifle Association, Air Force Association, American Medical Association, American Postal Workers Union, Farm Bureau Federation, Latex Foam Rubber Council, American Jewish Congress, Paper Bag Institute, Fergus Falls Chamber of Commerce, Florida Dairy Products Association, Environmental Defense Fund, Church League of America, and thousands of other national, international, regional, state, and local organizations.

As interest groups attempt to persuade government functionaries and the public about problems, opportunities, and policy options, in what ways is the intelligence of policy making affected? And what are the consequences for popular control of governmental problem solving?

WHO ARE THEY?

The term *interest group* is not at all precise. The largest single major category of interest group in democratic political systems—business enterprises—is no group in the ordinary sense. Such "groups" actually are hierarchically organized bureaucracies, managerial teams run from the top by a few officers. Even in a large corporation, a small number of executives wholly determines its interest-group activities, while the views of employees or stockholders generally are irrelevant to political activities. The same is true to a lesser extent of many other organizations active in politics, so the word *group* does not adequately describe all the kinds of organizations seeking to influence public policy.

Some of the participants in policy making who perform what is ordinarily called interest-group activity actually are individuals, not groups at all. Equivalent in their activities to interest groups are some private individuals of great wealth or high public standing: Donald Trump before his fall, Albert Einstein, and Henry Kissinger, for example. They operate like interest groups, using their funds and their voices to pull policy in directions they desire; and their influence raises the same questions as do the activities of organized groups. Ross Perot is the most recent example.

The study of interest groups now also identifies government officials, their associations, and their departments or agencies as playing interest-group roles. The Joint Chiefs of Staff play an interest-group role in influencing Congress. Reciprocally congressional committees and individual members of Congress try to influence the Department of Defense—say, to induce it to locate a military installation in a particular congressional district. To refer to government officials as members of interest groups seems odd. But, terminology aside, the point is that official policy-influencing activity often is not very different from that of private interest groups—as when a legislator joins with a lobbyist in a luncheon attempt to influence another member of Congress. As one study put it, "Lobbying on behalf of its own interests, controlling important appointments and resources, the executive branch of the federal government may be the most powerful lobby in the nation's capital."[4]

Very loosely, then, interest-group activities are interactions through which individuals and private groups not holding government authority seek to influence policy, together with those policy-influencing interactions of government officials that go well beyond the direct use of their authority. These activities play indispensable roles in policy making, and they also make very serious trouble. Let us look into both allegations.

INDISPENSABILITY OF INTEREST-GROUP ACTIVITY

Interest-group activities are generally believed to constitute an exercise of free thought, speech, petition, and assembly and hence the exercise of those liberties for which liberal democracy was established. The right of assembly implies the right to organize groups, and the right of free speech suggests the right to organize fund-raising for the purpose of buying newspaper space and broadcast time. Whether business corporations and other large institutions necessarily should enjoy all of the same liberties originally intended for individual citizens is one of the major issues unsatisfactorily addressed to date in democratic theory and practice.

Whatever their contribution to liberty, interest groups also perform specific policy-making functions. Everyone knows that the activities of interest groups often distort policy making, an issue addressed later in this chapter. But interest groups also perform more positive functions.

Clarifying and Articulating What Citizens Want

Private interest groups sometimes create an informative exchange between the ordinary citizen and more knowledgeable leaders and staff. Some of this occurs via newsletters and other communications, ordinarily prepared by professional staff. Also, when elections are held for leadership posts in a union or other interest group, differences of opinion among the candidates can help educate ordinary members about issues facing the organization. How often this actually happens varies radically among groups and among members of each group.

In addition, interest groups are helpful and perhaps necessary for bringing diverse viewpoints, factual information, and other ideas into the policy-making process. Since the organizations help shape their members' views, it would be wrong to say that they simply express what their members

---

[4]Ronald J. Hrebenar and Ruth K. Scott, *Interest Group Politics in America,* 2nd ed. (Englewood Cliffs, NJ: Prentice Hall, 1990), p. 238.

want. But interest groups often champion sets of needs or desires that their leadership believes will be endorsed, or at least accepted, by most of the membership. In the case of business enterprises, of course, the top executives are able to dictate the group's position without worrying much about the "membership."

Forming a Feasible Agenda

Beyond simple articulation of citizens' and group leaders' views, the interest-group system performs another set of tasks that are not as well understood. The number of alternative policies that a government might pursue on any issue is at least as large as the number of citizens, each of whom might have his or her own idea of a good policy. No one could consider all these millions of policy alternatives, so the number of proposals must be reduced to a manageable few. If policies are to be shaped by popular will, the thinking of large numbers of people must be brought together, giving up their many diversities in favor of a commonality that satisfactorily unites many of them.[5]

Seen this way, interest-group activity does not simply set segmental or particular interests against common interests. Instead, it helps overcome an impossible diversity and conflict of individual interests. Interest groups do not accomplish this on their own since the mass media and other social processes also contribute to this winnowing and shaping process. But while interest groups do not, of course, bring all members of the political system to a single shared view, they help greatly in structuring the conflicts.

The details vary greatly among political systems. In European systems where interests align closely with powerful political parties,

> interest groups have been instrumental in the shaping of party ideologies and programs. Thus in West Germany, the DGB (Confederation of German Trade Unions) played a major role in getting the SPD's endorsement of codetermination, of improvements in statutory medical insurance, and of anti-Nazi legislation.[6]

A qualification. To describe interest groups in these ways somewhat overstates the extent to which they are policy instruments of the public at large. Many people find themselves in interest groups for reasons having little to do with policy making. Thus, workers join unions largely for

---

[5]Nancy L. Schwartz, *The Blue Guitar: Political Representation and Community* (Chicago: University of Chicago Press, 1988) offers a penetrating discussion of tensions between pursuit of particular interests and development of a broader, shared sense of political community.

[6]William Safran, "Interest Groups in Three Industrial Democracies: France, West Germany, and the United States," in Fred Eidlin, ed., *Constitutional Democracy: Essays in Comparative Politics* (Boulder, CO: Westview, 1983), pp. 315–43, quote from p. 333.

nonpolitical reasons such as higher wages and job security. Group services, rather than the desire to influence policy, often draw members to private interest groups; the American Medical Association, for example, helps to protect physicians against malpractice suits.

Even citizens who affiliate with a private interest group because of its policy activity may not live up to the ideal picture: Rather than seeking to become informed and have an influence over policy, some citizens may rely on interest groups as another device for escaping the task of policy making. Not content with simply delegating proximate policy making to officials, such citizens also delegate to organized groups the task of watching and influencing the officials. In this respect, large and professionalized groups may promote a more passive rather than a more energetic type of grassroots democracy. Ordinary members of the Sierra Club or similar organizations probably learn more about environmental issues as a result of communications sent to them (partly for the purpose of raising money to support professional staff); but the members do not actually have to *do* anything except pay an annual membership fee.

Monitoring Governance

The surveillance function of interest groups is, in some eyes, their principal one: They blow the whistle. In environmental policy, the EPA routinely fails to comply with timetables and other announced congressional intentions.[7] The Natural Resources Defense Council (NRDC) and Environmental Defense Fund (EDF) just as routinely sue EPA in federal court and get judges to order the agency into action. The NRDC and EDF likewise maintain close relationships with Senate and House staff on the relevant committees and subcommittees, they testify at congressional hearings, and they even draft proposed legislation to correct perceived deficiencies in existing environmental law.

Interactive Problem Solving

Interest-group interactions with the bureaucracy make an important contribution to social problem solving by helping to cope with the great complexity of the governmental agenda. Voting can handle only a few of the many issues that government must decide, and even a legislature can handle only a small fraction of the points that must be decided. So delegation of authority to a department or bureau chief often becomes the most effective way to settle a policy issue.

---

[7]Daniel A. Mazmanian, *Beyond Superfailure: America's Toxic Policy for the 1990s* (Boulder, CO: Westview, 1992); Michael S. Greve and Fred L. Smith, *Environmental Politics: Public Costs, Private Rewards* (New York: Praeger, 1992).

But what if the official responds to too few of the varied interests of a disparate citizenry? To guard against this, a variety of devices may be established to compel an administrator to interact widely with specified other officials and private interest groups before making a choice of policy. The official may be required, for example, to take the problem to an interdepartmental committee, or to gain the consent of certain business groups or other private organizations whose interests or expertise bear on the issues. Or informal rules established by custom may require the official to work out a settlement among several clienteles, as when a regulatory commission seeks agreement for its price setting from the regulated industry, its labor unions, possibly a consumer group, and another agency responsible for fiscal or wage policy. In any case, interaction among those representing a variety of interests makes the delegated decision that no one official or agency can be trusted to reach alone.

This same process helps cope with complexity in a second way. As explained in earlier chapters, it often proves too time consuming or otherwise impossible to choose conclusively among competing policy options on the basis of analysis. When that occurs, some interactive procedure for political decision making must be employed to reach a judgment. By bringing diverse perspectives to bear on a problem, the interest-group system frequently can help evolve a policy choice that is more intelligent than what could be accomplished by a narrower policy-making process. As one observer of European policy processes puts it, a government "cannot substitute itself for the expertise of a group."[8] Of course, this capacity is undermined to the degree that relevant interests are not effectively represented, a nontrivial problem in most contemporary political systems.[9]

Coalition Building

Articulating interests is not enough to produce intelligent policy making, of course: There also must be a coalition capable of actually taking action. This is a special problem in the crippled American system, with its high hurdles to effective cooperation among government officials in House and Senate, presidency, judiciary, and state and local governments.[10] Though they also contribute to the obstructions, interest groups can be

---

[8]Safran, 1983, p. 329.

[9]Anne O'Hagan, *Do Men Represent Women?* (New York: National American Woman Suffrage Association, 1990); Wilma Rule and Joseph F. Zimmerman, *United States Electoral Systems: Their Impact on Women and Minorities* (New York: Greenwood Press, 1992).

[10]See John E. Chubb and Paul E. Peterson, eds., *Can the Government Govern?* (Washington, DC: Brookings, 1989), and James Sundquist, *Constitutional Reform and Effective Government* (Washington, DC: Brookings, 1987).

helpful in coalition building, as by assisting members of congressional committees in developing outside support for pending legislation.

In sum, interest groups help form a feasible agenda by clarifying and articulating what citizens want; they help monitor the actions of government, providing feedback directly to responsible officials, as well as complaining to other officials; they serve as a crucial source of information, not just of desires; and they help in building working coalitions. These roles are somewhat less important in nations with strong political party systems, since parties provide an alternative means of achieving some of the same ends.

SOURCES OF INTEREST-GROUP INFLUENCE

Interest-group activity undertaken by elected and appointed officials achieves an influence for readily understandable reasons: government functionaries have something to bargain with, since they are capable of employing their authority indirectly in many ways, and those with whom they interact are aware of this latitude. But how do nongovernmental groups achieve influence—is there more to it than votes and money, the two most widely recognized routes to influence?

Delivering the Vote

First, how important is the ability of groups to influence elections, to deliver the vote? Government officials are alleged to fear the adverse votes of members of private interest groups whom they disappoint, but many political scientists doubt the adequacy of this explanation. For if interest groups try to threaten a public official with their claims to control votes, "they are usually pointing an unloaded gun at the legislator," and he or she knows it.[11] Since many citizens' dispositions to vote for one party or another remain relatively fixed, an interest group leader trying to reward or punish an elected official often will have difficulty inducing much change in members' votes.

Additionally, members of a trade union or another large organization probably will not vote alike. Some vote as trade unionists, some as Catholics, some as conservatives, some as environmentalists, and so on. Nor is it a simple matter for a large interest group to communicate effectively with its members; it may be quite expensive and time consuming to persuade

---

[11]V. O. Key, Jr., *Public Opinion and American Democracy* (New York: Alfred A. Knopf, Inc., 1961), p. 522.

group leaders seek a lasting relation of confidence with a policy maker so they cannot very well threaten; for even if a functionary is unreceptive on one specific issue, interest-group lobbyists will want to maintain good relations in order to have his or her support in the future.

Organizations that single-mindedly pursue one issue, such as abortion, may find it much easier to deliver the vote of their single-minded membership when a multi-issue group like the AFL-CIO cannot. The success of the pro-gun lobbies in delaying and weakening gun control legislation has been striking, especially in the face of widespread concern about violent crime and with public opinion heavily favoring stricter gun laws.

For local elections, organized groups sometimes can exert a very powerful influence, as when school board elections are won by candidates endorsed by a teachers' union. And anti-tax organizations sometimes galvanize public sentiment against particular candidates or against state bond issues.

The effect of interest groups on elections varies greatly among nations. In highly unionized West Germany, labor has been relatively powerful through its connection with the Social Democratic Party; the 1992 public employees strike which led to a substantial wage increase suggests that labor's influence may be sustained in the reunified Germany.[12] In marked contrast, Japanese labor interests have been virtually shut out of government for the period since World War II because of their support for the toothless Socialist party, which does not win enough seats to have influence in government. In Britain, labor was shut out of government during the Thatcher era and was too divided to play a very constructive role in policy making even when the Labour Party controlled Parliament off and on in previous decades. In contrast, business has had a strong influence through support of conservative parties in each of these nations.

Campaign Funds

Only one step removed from delivering the vote, another familiar kind of interest-group influence is providing campaign financing for candidates. "They mention in their letters they are officers of such and such association," says a congressman. "All they have to say is if I do what they want,

---

[12]"In West Germany, the Confederation of German Trade Unions (DGB) has always kept the door open to the Christian Democratic Union (CDU) (and its labor-wing), so that the Social Democratic Party (SPD) does not take union support for granted." Safran, "Interest Groups in Three Industrial Democracies," p. 328. The relationship between Italian labor unions and parties is discussed in Joseph LaPalombara, *Democracy, Italian Style* (New Haven, CT: Yale University Press, 1987).

they're in a position to get some campaign funds for me."[13] Potential candidates who cannot find an ally in at least one major interest group often cannot, for lack of finance, run successfully. Hence, legislatures fill with members already disposed, without much prompting, to at least listen carefully to the concerns of those who helped them win office.

Many observers have expressed great concern about the rise of political action committees (PACs) and about their effects on campaigns. There were 4,157 registered PACs by 1986, contributing $130 million to congressional candidates in that year. But each PAC can contribute no more than $5,000 to one candidate; and while the absolute total funding they command is huge, individuals still account for 60 percent of all money raised by House candidates and 75 percent of the funds for Senate campaigns. Political action committees favor incumbents and thereby contribute to the problem of low turnover in Congress, especially the House; but contributions from individuals also go disproportionately to incumbents.[14]

Because PAC donations must be reported to the Federal Election Commission, data has been available for attempting to trace the relationship between donation patterns and congressional voting. The most careful studies to date generally find that PAC funding does not appear to have strong across-the-board impacts on legislators' votes. On broad national issues where political ideology is at stake and where the press is attentive, recipients of PAC dollars generally do not tilt much toward the donor's desired policies, if they are not already ideologically disposed in that direction.[15] A partial exception is where business and labor join together, as on trucking legislation, trade policy, and some types of environmental regulation perceived to be costly to business and to threaten union jobs. PAC influence also is common on issues with low visibility, and in the early stages of the legislative process when the media and watchdog groups are not very attentive. PAC gifts can be quite influential on specialized issues, moreover, especially if no other organized interests are in opposition.

The policy errors leading to the savings and loan bailout, for example, apparently resulted partly from campaign donations and near-corrupt financial relations between the U.S. League of Savings Institutions and Fernand St. Germain, longtime chair of the House Banking, Finance and Urban Affairs Committee. Said to have been "the undisputed godfather of the S&L industry," St. Germain allegedly got waterfront condos at bargain

---

[13]"Business Lobbying," *Consumer Reports* 43 (September 1978): p. 530.

[14]Sabato, 1987.

[15]Larry Sabato, *PAC Power: Inside the World of Political Action Committees,* rev. ed. (New York: W. W. Norton, 1985), pp. 122-59.

prices together with insider deals from savings banks.[16] He helped engineer near-deregulation of the savings and loan industry in 1982, which opened the door to wildly speculative—and ultimately disastrous—loans by previously conservative thrift institutions, even allowing S&L owners to make loans to themselves. In the Senate, deregulation was championed by Banking Committee Chair Jake Garn, who did not benefit financially but in whose honor savings institutions subsequently donated large sums to the nonprofit Garn Institute of Finance at the University of Utah, as did Drexel Burnham Lambert, the leading junk bond firm.[17]

Another lesser-known use of political money was the ability of interest groups to offer speaking fees and honoraria to legislators. This totalled $6.9 million in 1985, an average of more than $10,000 per member of Congress, but new congressional salary scales now have placed limits on the practice.[18]

Persuasion

As important as votes and money are, then, they are not quite as powerful as ordinarily assumed, and are not the full explanation for interest-group influence. Is influence perhaps also achieved for more "rational" reasons? By clarifying and articulating what people want, monitoring government's performance, and otherwise joining in the policy-making process, do interest groups somehow win an influential role for themselves?

The answer appears to turn on the central role of reasoned persuasion in political life, at which lobbyists sometimes develop great skill. Part of this is just cleverness: An aerospace firm that wants a new contract, for example, is not likely to emphasize how the contract would enlarge its profits. Instead it will lobby on some related ground that appeals to relevant officials' known values: more jobs, or protection of industrial capacity for national defense. If enough political participants are clever, however, each looking to make their own desires compatible with those of others, the way is opened to finding sensible policies on which a working majority can agree. This obviously requires many groups, representing diverse angles on a problem, so that inaccurate or misleading claims put forward by one interest group are effectively disputed by other groups; when these conditions are approximated, a good purpose sometimes can be served even by

---

[16]Brooks Jackson, *Honest Graft: Big Money and the American Political Process* (New York: Alfred A. Knopf, 1988).

[17]For further details on the controversy, see Edward J. Kane, *The S&L Mess: How Did it Happen?* (Washington, DC: Urban Institute Press, 1989), and R. Dan Brumbaugh, *Thrifts Under Siege: Restoring Order to American Banking* (Cambridge, MA: Ballinger, 1988).

[18]"The 1985 Honoraria Scorecard," *Common Cause Magazine* 12 (July-August 1986): 42; and Sheila Kaplan, "Join Congress—See the World," *Common Cause Magazine* 12 (September-October 1986): 17–23.

interest groups' somewhat manipulative and not fully sincere efforts at persuasion of others.

There is ample evidence that communications from interest groups often do serve an enlightenment function. A study of foreign-trade policy making found members of Congress heavily dependent on help from interest groups in analyzing how the legislators' own values would be affected by pro-business policies.[19] As a state legislator expressed it, lobbyists

> can study and present the issues concisely—the average legislator has no time or inclination to do it, and wouldn't understand bills or issues without them. A professional lobbyist in ten minutes can explain what it would take a member two hours to wade through just reading bills.[20]

One reason lobbyists tend to specialize and work with particular committees and their staffs is that "in time and with regular contact, lobbyists have the opportunity to prove that their information is reliable."[21] The effectiveness of informed persuasion is testified to also by the fact that

> no tactic is considered more effective by lobbyists than personally presenting their case to a member of Congress in a private meeting. [It is] an opportunity to press the case home and make him or her truly *understand* the virtue of the group's position. Washington representatives know that being seen as a good source of information is their entree back into the office.[22]

Asked to explain how their group's time and resources are expended,[23] interest group representatives in Washington put three types of persuasion at the top of their lists: (1) contacting government officials directly to present the group's point of view; (2) testifying at hearings; and (3) presenting research results or technical information.[24]

The important role played by partisan analysis helps explain the extraordinary effectiveness of some interest-group campaigns directed not at legislators or administrators but at the courts. By petitioning the courts to reconsider judicial doctrines affecting important questions of policy, the National Association for the Advancement of Colored People (NAACP)

[19]R. A. Bauer, I. de Sola Pool, and L. A. Dexter, *American Business and Public Policy* (New York: Atherton Press, 1963).

[20]J. C. Wahlke, H. Eulau, W. Buchanan, and L. C. Ferguson, *The Legislative System* (New York: John Wiley & Sons, Inc., 1962), p. 338.

[21]Jeffrey M. Berry, *The Interest Group Society* (Boston: Little, Brown, 1983), p. 183.

[22]Berry, 1983, pp. 186–87, emphasis added.

[23]Obviously lobbyists would downplay the more questionable sides of their work, such as inviting legislators on yachting trips.

[24]Kay Lehman Schlozman and John T. Tierney, *Organized Interests and American Democracy* (New York: Harper & Row, 1986), p. 151.

steadily won gains for blacks for a period of several decades in policy on housing, voting rights, transportation, education, and criminal justice. Gay rights, abortion, and other social policy issues likewise have been adjudicated at the behest of groups seeking to have their views incorporated into law. In the United States, the environmental movement likewise has achieved many of its gains through reasoned persuasion in the courts. These and other interest groups use partisan analysis to persuade judges that inconsistencies between established policies and constitutional rules call for corrective new policy.

Interest-Group Leaders as an Elite

The work of interest groups is sufficiently central to policy making that it makes sense to think of leaders of interest groups as members of a governing elite, along with high-level governmental functionaries and business executives. Interest-group leaders range from persons of great influence to persons merely busy rather than influential. But if the term elite refers to groups that are small relative to the whole citizenry and that exercise greatly disproportionate political influence, the most influential interest-group leaders certainly would qualify.

This is especially true of those who share actual authority when governmental policy makers delegate responsibility for public policy making to private parties. This happens in wholesale fashion for many economic decisions in a market-oriented society, as discussed in chapter 1. But such delegation is not limited to business managers; committees of the American Bar Association, for example, not government officials, wrote the corporate laws of at least fifteen states. And many European political systems explicitly incorporate both labor and business in corporatist policy making.

TROUBLESOME ASPECTS OF INTEREST GROUPS

Because organized groups serve such indispensable political functions, contributing both to the intelligence of the policy-making process and to the diversity of viewpoints brought to bear in representative democratic systems, government functionaries grant participation in policy making to those perceived as spokespersons for social concerns entitled to consideration. The de facto "rule" is that to get into the game, an organization is required; beyond that, publicity and other activities of the organization may serve largely as rituals.[25] This highly favorable interpretation of interest groups,

---

[25]On the extraordinarily significant and still inadequately appreciated role of symbol and ritual in political life, usually as an alternative to social problem solving but sometimes an important boost to such problem solving, see Murray J. Edelman, *The Symbolic Uses of Politics* (Urbana: University of Illinois Press, 1985 [1964]).

suggesting great rationality in the system, must be balanced by attention to another darker side to the story. For although interest-group activity makes indispensable contributions to policy making, it also makes trouble.

Political Inequality

In no contemporary democratic system do interest groups equally represent all citizens. Ethnic minorities, women, consumers, poor people, and political radicals tend to be underrepresented among organized groups, while ethnic majorities, men, business, the affluent, and those seeking to preserve existing patterns of privilege tend to be overrepresented. This is less true in Norway than in the United States, but to some degree it is true everywhere.

Although the vote is distributed relatively equally in most nations, all the other instruments of control available to interest groups—analytical skills, money, and organizational skill and readiness—are distributed most unequally. At an extreme, a single wealthy person on his or her own can achieve the same political influence as a poorly financed mass organization, as the activities of Ross Perot make apparent.

Inequality among persons is sometimes gilded over by allegations that the many groups in a democratic system exercise a roughly equal influence in politics. If true, that would itself point to inequality. For if groups differing greatly in size, the mammoth AFL-CIO and the much smaller National Association of Manufacturers, actually exercised roughly equal political influence, that necessarily would mean that each member of the AFL-CIO had far less influence than each member of the smaller organization.

But interest groups do not and cannot exert equal influence. Neither does influence correspond with number of members. As discussed in great detail in chapter 8, business groups in particular tend to have the advantage of better organization and finance compared with most other organized interests. Members of the medical profession, for example, draw on advantages of organization and finance for interest-group activity, and they are accorded unusually large influence in certain areas of medical policy. Organizations potentially representing far greater numbers of citizens, like the Urban League or Common Cause, face tougher sledding. Of course, many potential interests never achieve effective organization because their potential members are not well enough off to finance it.

Nor are all groups who seek access accorded it in equal measure. For many decades, black groups were simply excluded from the benefit of recognition as legitimate organizations deserving attention. Even in a period of rising status for women, the rules of politics recognized by some public officials do not require them to attend to women's organizations with the same concern as for men's. Officials also disregard some group leaders through a tacit rule that cranks, fools, and troublemakers deserve no attention. Thoughtful dissidents may also be assigned to the same category, and ignored at great cost to intelligent policy making.

Hence, interest-group activity is a source of great political inequality that does not square with democratic norms.

Subordination of Common to Segmental Interests

Another concern is that interest groups may neglect the common welfare in pursuit of their own narrow or segmental concerns. Although a plausible allegation, this one calls for caution. Perhaps, strictly speaking, viewpoints shared by all do not exist. Even on something as universal as a concern for preventing nuclear warfare, people's opinions diverge on the circumstances in which they would want to survive. And they differ on what risks they would choose to run (e.g., on whether President Bush should have risked chemical warfare over the Iraqi takeover of Kuwait). This does not deny the existence of widespread desires, such as those to avoid economic depression, to clean up the environment, or to improve education. But these hopes are so widely shared that they are not much disputed, and political disagreements generally focus on narrower, less agreed-on aspects of the issues. In other words, interest-group activity emphasizes differences rather than commonalities.[26]

This emphasis may make increasing trouble in the future. In the past, policy making was occupied mostly with "Who gets what?" issues: taxation, labor relations, farm policy, and industrial regulations. A few issues like national defense always have raised questions about the general welfare, of course; but policy making has shifted significantly in that direction in recent decades. New common issues have appeared in arms control, energy conservation, environmental protection, and international trade, among others. If the interest-group system was well suited for the older-style, segmental issues—and the critics doubt even that—it may cope badly with the newer problems on whose solution depends the welfare of all.[27]

Still, much interest-group activity pursues not narrow, self-serving desires but visions of a common interest. Opponents of nuclear power plants, advocates of a tough foreign-policy line toward Iraq or Nicaragua, proponents of reform of public education, and organizations like Mothers Against

[26]On concerns about excessive segmentation in bureaucratic politics, see Douglas Yates, *Bureaucratic Democracy: The Search for Democracy and Efficiency in American Government* (Cambridge: Harvard University Press, 1982), esp. pp. 105–19.

[27]Segmental interests often do present worthy moral and legal claims, of course. We would consider intolerable a political system that pursued common interests to the exclusion of segmental interests. The liberal democratic tradition applauds diversity in interest, opinion, and activity. Moreover, the deprived segments of the population need opportunities to pursue their segmental interests, as discussed in Iris Marion Young, "Polity and Group Difference: A Critique of the Ideal of Universal Citizenship," in Cass R. Sunstein, ed., *Feminism and Political Theory* (Chicago: University of Chicago Press, 1990), pp. 117–41.

Drunk Driving perceive themselves as battling for the common interest. As the point was once put, "The members of the American League to Abolish Capital Punishment were not a group of people in danger of being hanged."[28]

Too Many Veto Points?

To grant that interest groups often pursue some vision of the public interest does not say that the consequences of their efforts will be positive. Environmental groups holding out for stringent regulations on acid rain scuttled a compromise plan in 1987, resulting in no plan at all for additional years. Business routinely obstructs policies, as when automobile manufacturers in 1990 convinced Congress to abandon a bill requiring new cars to achieve an average of 40 miles per gallon by the year 2000. Labor unions sometimes obstruct efforts to make a nation's economy more competitive in global trade. The list could be extended.

This conflict between broad and narrow interests connects with the way democratic political systems are designed, specifically with rules dispersing the authority to veto or stop a policy initiative. A minority of members can stop the House or Senate from acting, in part because committees with a relatively few members are delegated the authority to consider legislation on behalf of the entire body. Once legislation passes one house, the other half of the Congress can kill it simply by inaction. Presidents veto, the judiciary holds up administrative action, and the federal-state-local distribution of authority routinely slows down or altogether derails problem-solving efforts.

Few of these barriers are so severe in other nations, but policy making in all democratic political systems is partly crippled by veto authority distributed outside government, especially that granted to business. As detailed in chapter 8, businesses are legally protected in their right to say no to government on many issues, and they use a combination of property rights and political might to obstruct policies on environmental pollution, energy shortage, unemployment, and other matters when action is perceived to disadvantage business.

Because vetoes are broadly distributed, interest groups converge on government functionaries and others who can exercise vetoes. To stop a policy move, it is necessary to influence only one of the many persons or bodies that can exercise a veto. To move a policy ahead, in contrast, a group must influence all political sources of veto. It is little wonder, then,

---

[28]E. E. Schattschneider, *The Semisovereign People* (New York: Holt, Rinehart, and Winston, Inc., 1960), p. 26. Also see Andrew S. McFarland, *Common Cause: Lobbying in the Public Interest* (Chatham, NJ: Chatham House Publishers, 1984).

that interest groups often obstruct policies required to deal with arms control and other shared interests on the modern political agenda.

This broad distribution of veto powers in democracies reflects their historical concern with personal liberty rather than with popular control or effective policy. Fearful that governments might intervene excessively, the designers of democratic systems permitted many participants, both governmental and nongovernmental, to stop the initiatives of government functionaries. This decision may have been wise, but they bought such protection for individual liberty at a high price, a price that appears to be rising in an era when collective problems have risen high on humanity's agenda. If vetoes can stop policy initiatives at many points, groups of citizens can control their government only when they want it to *desist*. Not even a large majority may be able to systematically and routinely control it when they want it to act.[29]

---

[29]A related argument concerning the need for a public sphere more capable of acting effectively is James A. Morone, *The Democratic Wish: Popular Participation and the Limits of American Government* (New York: Basic Books, 1990).

PART III

BROADER INFLUENCES ON POLICY MAKING

Chapter 8

The Position of Business in Policy Making

In addition to the formidable complications and obstructions from conventional electoral and governmental sources discussed in the preceding chapters, policy making also faces extra-governmental obstructions to intelligent, democratic steering of society. One of the most important of these is the business sector's influence over public policy.

A PRIVILEGED POSITION FOR BUSINESS?

As explained in chapter 1, business constitutes something of a rival system of public policy making, one in partial competition with the governmental system. Corporate executives and those they hire, in conjunction with consumers, make many of the consequential choices that construct our ways of life: Suburbs, automobiles, television and consumer electronics, the shift of manufacturing jobs overseas, and the rise of agribusiness to replace family farms have been shaped largely by the initiative of businesses and the technologies they deploy.[1] For example, threats to the ozone layer from chlorofluorocarbons

---

[1]This chapter is drawn in part from Charles E. Lindblom, *Politics and Markets: The World's Political-Economic Systems* (New York: Basic Books, 1977).

resulted in part from choices by General Electric and other large manufacturers to promote electric refrigerating equipment instead of natural gas systems that used a different refrigerant chemical.[2]

Thus businesses would play a unique and powerful role in the overall scope of public policy making even if corporate executives never exercised any influence over elections, political activities, or governmental actions. But they do, of course. The leadership role that business has in the economy gives executives of large corporations an unusual kind and degree of influence over governmental policy making. The logic is simple. Business managers perform economic functions essential to all of us: housing must be built, food processed, jobs made available, factories built and operated, people and goods transported. If these and similar activities falter, recessions and personal distress follow—as when loss of sales to imports led American steel, automotive, and other industries to throw several million workers out of their jobs in the past two decades.[3]

Government officials know that failure of businesses to maintain high employment—what is called a recession—will upset voters more quickly and more surely than just about anything else, as illustrated by President Bush's plummeting popularity and defeat by Bill Clinton. Since irate voters tend to throw incumbents out of office, an elected government cannot expect to survive in the face of widespread or prolonged distress. Extreme economic disorganization sometimes not only evicts officials in power but also can overthrow an entire regime or form of government, as some Americans believed possible during the Great Depression of the 1930s. Consequently, government policy makers show constant concern about business performance. As a business lobbyist puts it, "Jobs, payroll, economic growth—this is awfully important. A Congressman reacts positively to anything that affects jobs, growth in his district."[4]

But the rules of the market system set sharp limits on government's control of business. Although governments can prohibit certain activities, even the Japanese government cannot positively command corporate executives to perform the functions desired from them.[5] A business manager creates new jobs and otherwise performs only if he or she voluntarily decides to do so in the pursuit of profit. How then can a government official be reasonably confi-

---

[2]The crucial decisions are summarized by historian of technology Ruth Schwartz Cowan, in *More Work for Mother: The Ironies of Household Technology from the Open Hearth to the Microwave* (New York: Basic Books, 1983), pp. 128–45.

[3]Carolyn C. Perrucci et al., *Plant Closings: International Context and Social Costs* (New York: Aldine De Gruyter, 1988).

[4]"Business Lobbying," *Consumer Reports* 43 (September 1978):529.

[5]But the Japanese Ministry of International Trade and Industry came close in the 1950s; See Chalmers Johnson, *MITI and the Japanese Miracle: The Growth of Industrial Policy, 1925–75* (Palo Alto: Stanford University Press, 1982).

dent that managers will discharge the functions that keep an economy afflu-ent? The answer is, by making sure that business executives find it advanta-geous to do so.

One might think that, because opportunities for profit lie everywhere, business executives will certainly find inducement to perform their functions. Yet not even Adam Smith believed they would inevitably do so if left to their own devices. The well-known business cycle in market-oriented economies goes through periodic slowdowns, as during the recession of 1990–92; in many parts of the world, such as much of Africa, economic growth usually is slow. Businesses perform their functions well only when governments develop sup-porting policies that induce investments, assist with aggressive marketing of exports, and otherwise promote a business climate conducive to profitable ac-tivities. In part because Japanese government agencies control much of the financial capital available to banks, and through them to manufacturing in-dustries, the government is in a better position to induce "voluntary" compli-ance than are most other governments of market-oriented societies.[6] But in-duce it must.

Inducements take a wide variety of forms: subsidized transportation and banking facilities, outright cash subsidies, protected markets, low business taxes, military protection for foreign investments, employee training pro-grams, research services, and tax writeoffs for investments in plant and equip-ment. One should add to the list tariffs, minimum price maintenance, pur-chases of surpluses, sharing of costs of new technologies, as well as many routine services like weather reporting, mapping, and policing. As part of its effort to spur economic recovery in Britain through policies favorable to busi-ness, the Thatcher government undertook a "step by step but steady pro-gramme to curb the power of unions."[7] The German Ministry of Trade acts so deferentially toward business that it even allowed export to Libya of facilities capable of manufacturing poison gas.

The business sector does not receive everything it asks for, of course, sometimes even suffering bitter defeats, such as the National Clean Air Coali-tion's victory in the 1990 Clean Air Act revisions.[8] But beneath the nontrivial ups and downs of business influence is an underlying pattern, which is that government functionaries must listen to business executives with special care,

[6]See John Zysman, *Government, Markets and Growth* (Ithaca: Cornell University Press, 1983).

[7]Graham K. Wilson, *Business and Politics: A Comparative Introduction,* 2nd ed. (Cha-tham, NJ: Chatham House Publishers, 1990), p. 81.

[8]Gary C. Bryner, *Blue Skies, Green Politics: The Clean Air Act of 1990* (Washington, DC: Congressional Quarterly Press, 1992). Changing patterns of political victories and defeats by particular industries and by the business sector as a whole are traced in David Vogel, *Fluctuating Fortunes: The Political Power of Business in America* (New York: Basic Books, 1989).

care reserved for no other group in society. Government officials must find out what business needs even if corporate executives do not take the trouble to speak for these requirements; must give managers enough of what they need to motivate production, jobs, and growth.

In each of these ways, governments award to business managers a privileged position in policy making. Elected officials often end up giving business needs precedence over concerns that citizens express through electoral and interest-group channels. This counterintuitive outcome even makes good political sense: Neglect of business brings stagnation or unemployment, at great peril to officials in power; in contrast, citizen and interest-group demands often can be evaded or deflected, given the looseness of popular control over officials.

A privilege is not necessarily unwarranted, of course, and many people believe that the privileges accorded to the business sector are entirely appropriate.

THE RANGE AND KINDS OF CONTROL

Business managers will ask for more than they need and more than they expect to win. Whatever they want, government officials must consider. And it is very difficult to test whether business actually needs what it asks for, since a conclusive answer is only available after the fact: does the denial result in restricted business activity and increased unemployment? Thus a luxury tax passed in the United States in 1990 appeared to cut into sales by yacht builders, furriers, and jewelers; when some of their businesses subsequently failed, a clamor went up to repeal the tax. As a former Du Pont executive observes, "the strength of the position of business and the weakness of the position of government is that government needs a strong economy just as much as business does, and the people need it and demand it even more."[9]

Sometimes business managers threaten dire consequences if government policy does not meet their demands. Usually, however, they do not do so; elected and appointed government functionaries become accustomed to exercising a solicitous concern for the needs of business. Thus, the White House Council on Competitiveness achieved notoriety during Vice President Dan Quayle's chairmanship by unilaterally setting aside provisions of the Clean Air Act on the grounds that they interfered with the economy.

Benefits to business fall into two categories. The largest category consists of substantive policies helpful to business—those on taxes, for example. The second category consists of arrangements allowing businesspeople to share in

[9]Harold Brayman, *Corporate Management in a World of Politics* (New York: McGraw Hill, 1967), p. 57.

policy making explicitly and directly, as when government allows business associations to veto regulatory appointments or when business advisory groups attach to government departments. For example, the Nixon White House asked for industry opinions on appointments to the Federal Trade Commission and to the Federal Communications Commission, but it refused to hear consumer groups.

Businesspeople's privileged communication with government officials makes persuasion easier than it is for other citizens. Sometimes there is an explicit quid pro quo, as when a corporation agrees to locate or remain in a city only after bargaining with the municipal government over tax concessions. While paying $70 million in fines for violations of military procurement contract regulations, for example, General Electric in the early 1990s was attempting to extract from its longtime home city of Schenectady, New York, a 50 percent reduction in property taxes, at a time when the city already was hard hit by GE layoffs and restructurings.

More often business managers strike no explicit bargain. Government instead offers a benefit in hopes of a response. Government functionaries may come to believe that new investments will lag unless interest rates decline; so the monetary authorities reduce rates in hopes of a reciprocal increase in investment. No corporation promises anything in return, and they may or may not respond as the Federal Reserve or Bank of England intends.

Actual formal authority is sometimes conferred on managers and their organizations, as when regulations or appointments require clearance by certain companies or associations. As an observer remarked of a business association participating in British policy making, "It looked and acted like a government department."[10] In the United States, a congressional committee found excessive business participation in the Business and Defense Services Administration: "In operation, the organizational arrangements of BDSA have effected a virtual abdication of administrative responsibility on the part of the Government officials in charge of the Department of Commerce in that their actions in many instances are but the automatic approval of decisions already made outside the Government in business and industry."[11]

Japanese trade associations "sometimes act on behalf of government, saving the government time [and] resources."[12] The Japanese Federation of Economic Organizations (the *Keidanren*) has negotiated trade agreements with a number of nations, for example, and it was an automobile manufacturers' trade association that negotiated the "voluntary" agreements with the U.S.

---

[10]Louise A. Kohlmeier, *The Regulators* (New York: Harper & Row, Publishers, 1969), p. 49; Stephen Blank, *Industry and Government in Britain* (Lexington, MA: D.C. Heath and Co., 1973), pp. 67–70, 211.

[11]Grant McConnell, *Private Power and American Democracy* (New York: Alfred A. Knopf Inc., 1967), p. 271.

[12]Wilson, *Business and Politics*, p. 150.

and British governments to reduce sales of Japanese automobiles. In Austria, employers' organizations actually are granted legal powers to limit the pay increases that member businesses are allowed to grant.[13]

Businesspeople usually exercise control without great expenditure of attention or deliberation. They simply operate under circumstances in which both they and government officials know that continued performance depends on business indulgences, benefits, privileges, and incentives. As already noted, if government provides enough, they may perform well; if not, the economy will languish. Under those circumstances, government officials routinely and constantly attend to the needs of business.

At points during the 1992 presidential election campaign, for example, outsider H. Ross Perot and a bevy of Democratic challengers all were trying to outdo avowedly pro-business President Bush in claiming to know how to induce businesses to provide jobs and economic well-being.

Business Privileges Unique?

Do government policy makers grant similar participation in the making of policy to any other large category of citizens? Although organized labor is sometimes seen as roughly equal to business, it is not. Because of unions' ability to block wage-control policies by threat of widespread strikes, in many nations unions have won key participatory roles in policy areas dealing with wages and working conditions. Their influence extends to social policy issues in much of Europe, Australia, and other nations with powerful socialist parties. But not even in Scandinavia do unions enjoy across-the-board influence comparable to the range of issues on which business is consulted.

This is partly because workers have a harder time than business managers in withholding performance of their functions until they get what they want. When there is a general strike, as in Poland during protests against communist rule in 1989, workers may be able to shut down an economy and topple a government. It is rare that so many workers act in unison, however, and when only a relatively few workers go on strike they usually are not very powerful—as witnessed by the quick action against striking rail workers in the United States in 1992. With a few exceptions like garbage collectors in New York City, most workers need wages even more urgently than society needs their services; so a business can operate in low gear for a lot longer than workers can afford to stay off the job. Nor do a few thousand (or even a million) dissatisfied wage earners pose a threat of recession. Hence it is not obvious to many government officials why they should invite workers' representatives such as union officials into most aspects of governmental policy making.

---

[13]Berad Maria, "Austria: The Paradigm Case of Liberal Corporatism," in Wyn Grant, ed., *The Political Economy of Corporatism* (London: Macmillan, 1985).

This is not to deny that a good argument can be mounted for being more concerned with workers' needs, performance, and participation in both corporate and governmental policy making. The sharp contrast between workers' performance at most General Motors' manufacturing plants and at Honda, Nissan, and other Japanese plants in the U.S. is testimony to the importance of creative, responsible, hard-working employees. Since workers are among those most affected by corporate policy making, moreover, a great many observers argue that they deserve to participate influentially in business decision making in an economic democracy.[14] Policy making in government might be well served by granting a substantial role to union officials or others who speak on behalf of workers' aspirations. At present, however, in many nations unions are perceived to operate largely for the benefit of their own members, and protecting workers is considered a less essential function for society than those performed by business enterprises, especially in nations like the United States where most of the workforce is not unionized.

For all these reasons, unions are no match for business in competition for influence in governmental policy making.

ADDITIONAL FORMS OF BUSINESS INFLUENCE

A hiatus remains in the argument. It looks as though two quite separate control processes operate on government officials: customary electoral controls (votes, interest groups) and business controls. Do the two conflict? If so, what happens?

In the affluent nations some mechanism usually resolves the conflict, since businesses apparently get enough of what they need to induce relatively high levels of investment and employment. Although defeated on particular issues, businesspeople generally perform well enough to avoid intolerable unemployment and other economic disorder—evidence that they receive sufficient indulgences in public policy. Perhaps electoral controls, then, are too weak to challenge business controls? Or are electoral controls somehow manipulated so that they support rather than conflict with business controls?

Although business modifies its demands somewhat to avoid collision with electoral demands on government, becoming more tolerant of environmental regulation, for example, the principal reconciliation between the two control systems comes about by adjusting electoral controls to make them consistent with those of business. Businesspeople bring electoral controls into line by entering into interest-group, party, and other electoral activities and achieving disproportionate influence.

---

[14]Robert A. Dahl, *A Preface to Economic Democracy* (Berkeley: University of California Press, 1985).

Business does not enter into these activities on a parity with others from consumer, labor, professional, and veterans groups. These others depend on electoral activity as their main source of influence over government. For businesspeople electoral activity merely *supplements* the controls already exercised through their privileged position in government. They enter into electoral activities simply to strengthen their privileged position, to bend electoral controls toward the policies they seek through their more important privileged controls. The looseness of electoral controls often permits officials to do what business wants in any case, so electoral controls do not have to be bent very far.

Specifically, how do business managers bring electoral controls to support the privileged position of business?

Persuasion of Citizens

Over many years, citizens have been told that their own jobs and prosperity would be jeopardized by "antibusiness" policies citizens might consider demanding through electoral activity: higher taxes on business instead of on themselves, for example. Likewise common are claims that businesses cannot afford the expenses of making mines and factories safer: For decades the United Mine workers did not dare press for enforcement of safety legislation for fear that jobs would be endangered. Business spokespersons also caution against requiring full compensation for employees injured on the job, against regulation of misleading advertising, against tighter controls over consumer fraud. Above all, perhaps, citizens are discouraged from seeking wage increases to bring a significantly larger share of the national income to low paid workers.[15]

On many of these points business executives gradually have yielded. But even today they enjoy what by some standards are extraordinary tax favors. Workplaces are less safe than they easily could be, as are consumer products. Despite stricter labeling requirements and other truth-in-advertising laws, it remains legal to misrepresent many products to consumers.[16] Business still greatly pollutes the environment even after decades of tightening controls. And earnings remain grossly unequal, with salaries and bonuses of the highest paid executives totaling $10 million or more, a thousand times higher than the earnings of those receiving the minimum wage. Why do so few citizens (wisely or foolishly) draw the conclusion that, if policies like these must be accepted because of business needs in a private enterprise market system, it would be

---

[15]On the essentially unchanging shares of business receipts going to labor, see Vogel, *Fluctuating Fortunes,* p. 283. More generally, on the lack of income improvement for lower-middle and poor people who make up the bottom 40 percent of the American public, see Benjamin I. Page, *Who Gets What From Government* (Berkeley: University of California Press, 1983) and Nan L. Maxwell, *Income Inequality in the United States, 1947-1985* (New York: Greenwood, 1990).

[16]On the low efficacy of labeling, see Susan G. Hadden, *Read the Label: Reading Risk by Providing Information* (Boulder, CO: Westview Press, 1986).

better to experiment with modifications to the system? Why do they accept the *claims* of business and government officials rather than insisting on tight controls as an experiment to see if dire consequences really would follow?

Business managers join with government officials to assert that business demands are reasonable. Most government officials, the president included, assure the citizenry of their own concern for "the needs of business" and in so doing teach the public that, since business needs must be met for the sake of a sound economy, their own hands and the citizens' are tied. Business managers continually issue such warnings, their claims passed on in news stories and editorial comment alike that high taxes will hurt investment and jobs, or that ambitious mileage requirements for new automobiles will harm manufacturers' efforts to compete with imports. The claims sometimes have validity but usually are exaggerated.

Government functionaries join easily in such persuasive exercises because, given the rules of a market system, many business demands ask nothing unreasonable, and others look reasonable on the surface. The ordinary citizen must agree to give business demands priority over his or her own, unless willing to modify the market system and private enterprise more than most people are willing to contemplate seriously. Why do not more people consider bolder moves toward restructuring the privileged position of business?[17]

That very few people entertain such a possibility can be explained in part by their tendency to think of private enterprise and democracy as inseparable—indeed many think of their own liberties and private enterprise as inseparable. Business executives and government officials steadily reinforce this view. The easy confusion of private enterprise, democracy, and nation appears in declarations like that of a Secretary of the Interior, who proclaimed during the Bicentennial, "This is the year to wave the flag and wave the free enterprise flag."[18] A British industrial association similarly identified the interests of the whole society with the interests of business when it declared it would oppose subversion of "the security of Britain in general and British industry in particular."[19] Businesses make it a point to put their executives in leadership positions in public-interest organizations like the Red Cross and the United Fund. All this makes it difficult for a citizen to distinguish democracy from private enterprise; few are able to consider the possibility that business demands obstruct citizens' demands and that some aspects of the present business system may be an undemocratic element fitting oddly into a society aspiring to be more democratic.

The persuasive efforts of business spokespersons and government offi-

---

[17]Chapter 10 pursues that question in terms of the ways social institutions help forge human thinking and constraints on it.

[18]*The New York Times* (June 8, 1976):51.

[19]A. A. Rogow, *The Labour Government and British Industry* (Ithaca, NY: Cornell University Press, 1955), p. 146.

cials tend to remove important issues from policy debate. On fundamental issues pertaining to the structure of government and economy, a barrage of persuasion teaches citizens to accept corporate autonomy, the existing distribution of wealth, the limited authority of employees in business management, and close consultation between business and government as fundamental virtues of the established order not to be challenged. Consequently, they do not become policy issues.

Businesspeople do not limit their efforts to public declarations, propaganda, and public relations; they plunge into the whole range of political activity, becoming the most active citizens, and their corporations often become the most active private political organizations. Individuals and corporations contribute to campaign funds, put their own energies to work in political parties and interest groups, and organize to further the candidacies of persons favorable to them. In the words of a West German business representative, "This is not an alien world to the entrepreneur; it is his own. At stake for him is the leadership of the state."[20]

Advantages in Electoral Politics

Granting that through persuasion and electoral activities business managers would like to bring citizens' electoral demands into conformity with business goals, they might fail. That they largely succeed in Japan, Europe, and the United States follows from their three great advantages over all other groups.

Funds. No other interest group has disposable funds comparable to those of the business sector; they dwarf union or other interest-group resources. One study of lobbying on tax policy issues found that conservative and business-oriented groups like the U.S. Chamber of Commerce's Tax Policy Committee and the American Business Conference spent more than 20 times as much as did small, liberal organizations like the Public Citizens Tax Reform Group.[21]

Well over $100 million per year is spent by the business sector on institutional advertising, advertising that does not promote a product but a point of view. It ranges from Mobil Oil's paid public affairs ads on the Op-Ed page of *The New York Times* to "W. R. Grace Co.'s televised commentary, designed for the general public, on the abstract principles of freedom and small government, presented as background to a film of windsurfers succeeding and failing

[20]Quoted in Heinz Hartmann, *Authority and Organization in German Management* (Princeton: Princeton University Press, 1959), p. 229.

[21]Don A. Mele, "Organizations Seeking to Influence Tax Policy," *Tax Notes* 13 (September 21, 1981):627–636.

to negotiate cresting waves, in a visual analogy to the vicissitudes of the free market."[22]

The U.S. Chamber of Commerce, with a staff of 1,000 and a budget of $65 million, has become "the political arm, or club, of business. The network of 2,800 state and local Chambers of Commerce in cities and small towns across the country, the 210,000 corporations that are members, and the 1,400 professional and trade associations provide an ideal base for grass-roots lobbying, particularly when the issue before Congress is perceived as a threat by the business community."[23] Using its computerized data base of business executives, on a hot issue the Chamber can generate tens of thousands of telephone calls and other communications to members of Congress from their districts.

Most interest groups must finance their work out of contributions from personal income, but business interest-group activity does not. A curious and extraordinary arrangement from some perspectives, democracies permit one category of citizens, businesspeople, to finance their interest-group activity out of "public" funds—the receipts of business enterprises, especially the receipts of corporate enterprises.[24]

Turning corporate funds to political use runs throughout the liberal democracies but is most apparent in Japan. Politicians there spend about four times as much per citizen as do members of the U.S. Congress and so are even more pressed to raise funds. The result is predictable:

> Scandal is therefore endemic as politicians scramble for funds largely from business. The Lockheed scandal in the 1970s and the Recruit scandal in the 1980s were both reflections of a much more widespread pattern of business executives and LDP [Liberal Democratic Party] politicians exchanging favours. Both were followed by prosecutions, moral outrage and little fundamental reform.[25]

One of those forced out of office in 1987 due to scandal, Kiichi Miyazawa, became Prime Minister of Japan in 1991.

Available organizations.   A second great advantage of businesspeople in politics is in their organizations, already functioning and ready. Every corporate enterprise constitutes an interest group, as does a small business in local

[22]Thomas Byrne Edsall, *The New Politics of Inequality* (New York: W. W. Norton, 1984) p. 116.

[23]Edsall, *The New Politics of Inequality,* p. 124.

[24]The legal restrictions on corporate contributions to campaign funds are widely evaded. Many corporations also take the legal route of asking their executive personnel to make personal campaign contributions, which are legal. The corporation can adjust their pay or other payments with the effect of reimbursing them. See David W. Adamany and George E. Agree, *Political Money* (Baltimore: John Hopkins University Press, 1975).

[25]Wilson, *Business and Politics,* pp. 152–53.

politics. Ordinary citizens can organize political activity only if they are willing to pay a price in time, energy, and money. Corporate executives pay no such great price. They do not need laboriously and expensively to assemble a team of political activists: They can use those already on the payroll. Business managers' use of their own enterprises as political organizations has come to be common practice in the democracies. Not only are they well organized, but they have the requisite expertise to engage in the reasoned persuasion that is one of the most influential means of gaining access, building credibility, and winning influence.

Access. The third great advantage of businesspeople in electoral politics derives from the ease of access to elected and appointed government functionaries. Already engaged in routine and frequent discussion with government officials, already frequently called on for information and advice, when businesspeople turn to interest-group and campaign activity, doors stand open for them, with habits of consultation already established.

This is illustrated by defeat of a proposed consumer protection agency, with each influential legislator approached personally and warned (that the measure would cause economic damage) by the chief executive officer of a major corporation with political clout in the representative's district. Staff members of the Business Roundtable organized the lobbying campaign, as indicated by the following brief excerpts from a long meeting discussing how best to gain access to each congressperson: "OK, let's ask Sears about Gonzalez. . . . Well, Delaney's a character, but he was helpful as chairman of the Rules Committee. . . . Bristol-Myers is close to Delaney, let Bill Greif handle that. . . . Ask Alcoa if they'll do (Gaydos). . . . Ask Ferguson of General Foods to call Kirby of Westinghouse about Marks. . . . (To approach Al Gore of Tennessee), ask Lloyd Hand of TRW." The business reporter who recorded this session noted in his commentary that CEOs "can always get a hearing; busy politicians and bureaucrats will juggle their appointment books to see the head of General Motors or IBM. They practice the politics of persuasion on the highest levels."[26]

CONCLUSION

The influence of business on particular policy disputes obviously rises and falls in different eras. Even during periods of maximum influence businesses will not win every battle. And there is considerable conflict within the business sector, such as that between small and large business, between those competing

---

[26]Walter Guzzardi, Jr., "Business Is Learning How to Win in Washington," *Fortune* 97 (March 27, 1978): 52–58, quote from p. 53.

in global markets and those in protected markets, and between innovating and mature industries.[27]

There was an upsurge of environmental, consumer, and other public-interest organizations in the 1960s and 1970s; in response, businesses and their allies stepped up political activity, culminating in the elections of Reagan in the United States, Thatcher in Britain, and Kohl in Germany. Since that high water mark, business influence has ebbed somewhat.

But the underlying phenomenon remains unchanged: the business sector is structurally advantaged compared with other political interests. Overall, two scholars studying the "changing pressure community" in Washington found that despite many new organizations arising to represent the interests of consumers, the environment, the elderly, and minorities,

> the proportion representing the interests of business rose from 57 percent to 72 percent since 1960. The proportion of citizens' groups decreased from 9 percent to 5 percent of all organizations and the proportion representing labor plummeted from 11 percent to 2 percent.[28]

The political strength of business appears to grow when there is widespread concern about the strength of the economy and to decline when faith in the economy returns.[29] Over the long run, government regulation of business clearly has expanded. Along with new restrictions, however, the U.S. government administers many new financial supports to businesses through tax concessions, loan guarantees, and other subsidies: The savings and loan industry recently has become perhaps the largest such beneficiary ever, with the cost of the bailout projected to reach as much as $500 billion.

Gradual shifts in types and degrees of business privilege do not, in any case, affect the main line of analysis of this chapter. In market systems, since business performs only when induced to do so, government must follow policies that provide the necessary inducements. If the pattern of inducement alters somewhat decade to decade, the basic necessity remains.

Great consequences follow from this: The central role of business in politics renders the task of intelligent, democratic governmental policy making extremely difficult. When public interest groups and governments try to step in and ameliorate the pollution, workplace dangers, shoddy products, plant closings, or other public threats created by business decision making, three influential forces interfere. First, government officials fear that strict regulations may cripple a business or industry, causing even greater harm to workers,

---

[27]On conflict within the business sector, see Vogel, *Fluctuating Fortunes,* and Wilson, *Business and Politics,* for numerous examples.

[28]Kay Lehman Schlozman and John T. Tierney, *Organized Interests and American Democracy* (New York: Harper & Row, 1986), pp. 77–78.

[29]Vogel, *Fluctuating Fortunes.*

communities, and the society overall. Thus, without business executives ever having to lobby, donate, or even telephone a government official, the built-in logic of a market-oriented society will tend to slow down and weaken government actions that restrain business.

Second, many citizens share the fears of government officials concerning "excessive" restrictions on business. It does not take a degree in economics to recognize that workers' jobs depend on business hiring decisions. And almost everyone in a business-oriented culture has at least a dim perception of factors that influence the business climate. Even if government officials might favor strict regulation of business, then, electoral pressures may dissuade them.

Third, electoral and other political activity by business works to enlarge the fears of both government officials and ordinary citizens. It is impossible to determine just how government might behave toward business in the absence of political activity by business, because a high level of such activity has for so long been a routine feature of political life. Business executives and their allies endeavor energetically to convince citizens and government officials alike to increase support for business and to reject problem solving that would require costs and restrictions uncongenial to the business sector. Success in such persuasion or propaganda campaigns is all the more likely due to the disproportionate funds and other advantages available to business for electoral activity. Business executives and their sympathizers have the access, organization, expertise, and funds to move political actors toward pro-business policies.

The problem of how to bend business to better serve society is one of the fundamental challenges facing those who desire more intelligent and more democratic policy making (see chapter 12).

Chapter 9

Political Inequality

We have analyzed selected aspects of the problem of political inequality in earlier chapters. This chapter confronts the issue more fully, asking about the relationship of equality and democracy, the extent and origins of inequality, and the implications of inequality for effective policy making.

DEMOCRACY AND INEQUALITY

Strictly speaking, political inequality does not deprive citizens of control; it simply means that some citizens exercise more control than others do. The norm of political equality harks back to the axiom that democracy requires not simply responsiveness to citizens, but an equal distribution among them of capacities for exerting influence. Most democratic theorists have subscribed to this ideal because the alternatives are unpalatable: If not equality, then what *is* a justifiable distribution of privilege and influence?

One alternative recurrently proposed since Plato is that some set of benevolent guardians should exercise the lion's share of influence in policy making. Considering the many flaws of ordinary political functionaries and citizens, this notion is not without its attractions. In over 2,000 years of attempts by some of humanity's best minds, however, no one has been able to make a convincing case for any method of identifying those persons with the wisdom to serve as guardians, nor to explain how everyone else might be persuaded peaceably to follow the guardians' wishes.[1] The same problem confronts anyone proposing that one set of citizens—say, the more educated, or the more moral—should exercise disproportionate authority.

In our view, therefore, it is impossible to justify systematic deviations from political equality among all citizens.[2] Nevertheless, while most people give rhetorical support to the idea of equality, especially in America, the norm of equality actually does not command universal support. Favored groups often exhibit self-serving desires to protect their inegalitarian advantages, as in relations between whites and blacks or between wealthy and poor. Political equality and the goal of popular control over policy making may be questioned by those who want the better informed and educated citizens to exercise greater influence on policy making. And almost everyone wants some policy-making responsibility parceled out to especially competent decision makers: decisions on technology to scientists and engineers, on medical care to the medical profession, on monetary policy to bankers and economists, and so on. If they want political equality at all, most people probably want it only to control a few key decisions, such as those concerning who shall hold elected office, and perhaps those concerning broad policy directions.

Many people do not care greatly about equality or inequality, moreover, and believe that other considerations are more significant. Some want policy making to be highly adaptable, capable of innovation; conversely, others believe that the main problem of any society is simply to keep the social peace, and they ask only that policy making not rock the boat. Still others have a vision of an ideal society, such as one with minimal government, and for them the best policy-making system is one that will bring society closer to their ideal. At an extreme, some people may believe they know which policies are correct and incorrect, in which case they may opt for the policy-making system they think is most likely to reach correct policies. All such people may set equality and inequality aside as relatively unimportant.

Egalitarians themselves differ on the meaning of political equality. Does it call for the equal influence of all citizens on each piece of legislation? Or for equal say on the package of policies that a party might present to the voters? Or simply on choice of representatives who, after their election, can freely legislate as they think best? Does the equality principle apply merely to the vote, or also to equality in participation via interest groups and other forms of influence?

Thus, political equality does not stand as a generally accepted or as a

---

[1]For an extended analysis, see Robert A. Dahl, *Democracy and its Critics* (New Haven, CT: Yale University Press, 1989), pp. 65-79.

[2]For some very difficult matters concerning who is to be considered a "citizen" for purposes of a given policy, see Dahl, 1989, pp. 119-30.

TABLE 9–1. Projected Increases in Turnout from
Easing Registration Laws[4]

	TOTAL INCREASE
Whites	8.9 percent
Blacks	11.3
Less than high school education	10.4
High school	9.3
Some college	7.8
College graduate	5.6
Graduate school	2.8
Low income	10.1
Moderate income	8.7
High income	6.2

well-defined criterion for policy making; but it nevertheless is linked closely with our understanding of what would constitute a well-functioning democracy. The effects of inequality on the intelligence of governmental problem solving also turn out to be substantial.

PATTERNS OF UNEQUAL PARTICIPATION

One obvious source of political inequality is that many people do not vote. Among other causes of low voter turnout are voter registration laws, which reduce turnout in U.S. elections more than do the electoral laws of most other nations. An estimated 10 million additional votes would be cast in presidential elections if all states eliminated registration deadlines, allowed evening or Saturday registration, and took other steps to make it easier for citizens to register.[3] Strict registration requirements disadvantage all groups in the population, even the best educated and most affluent. But easier voter registration would especially help nonwhites, those with less education, and lower-income groups, as shown in Table 9–1.

Legally imposed inequalities aside, many citizens find little motivation to participate actively in politics. Fully one third of American citizens neither vote, join interest groups, communicate with their representatives, nor discuss

[3]Steven J. Rosenstone and Raymond E. Wolfinger, "The Effect of Registration Laws on Voter Turnout," pp. 54–86 in Richard G. Niemi and Herbert F. Weisberg, eds., *Controversies in Voting Behavior,* 2nd ed. (Washington, DC: Congressional Quarterly Press, 1984).

[4]Adapted from Rosenstone and Wolfinger, 1984, Table 4–4, p. 67. See also G. Bingham Powell, Jr., "Voting Turnout in Thirty Democracies: Partisan, Legal, and Socio-Economic Influences," in Richard Rose, ed., *Electoral Participation: A Comparative Analysis* (London: Sage, 1980); Raymond E. Wolfinger and Steven J. Rosenstone, *Who Votes?* (New Haven, CT: Yale University Press, 1980).

TABLE 9-2.   American Political Participation[5]

Voted in recent presidential elections	52 %
Voted in recent congressional elections	40
Persuaded others about vote choice	29
Contacted a government official about some issue	20
Attended political event in last three years	9
Gave money to a party or candidate	3

politics with their friends. Table 9-2 shows the pattern whereby millions of citizens effectively grant to others much greater influence than they keep for themselves.

Information, Analysis, and Education

One inequality among citizens appears in their information about political issues, including sharp differences in the extent to which people seek political information. The percentages engaging in various information-acquiring activities during recent American election campaigns are as follows:

	Yes	No
Watched political programs on television	50–90%	10–50%
Read newspaper articles about the election	70–80	20–30
Read about campaign in magazines	30–40	60–70

All nations display some political inequality, but few of the affluent Western nations display patterns like that of the United States. In Denmark and Norway, among the least unequal, more than 80 percent vote.

CAUSES OF INEQUALITY

Why are there these inequalities in information and in disposition to seek it? Among other causes, people differ in their capacity to understand and use information, both about issues and about the political process in Washington, London, or Paris. One early study estimated that for only about 16 percent of American voters was their vote related to an organized set of ideas. For another 45 percent, the vote was related to group benefits. For 23 percent, the vote was related vaguely to the nature of the times, such as the state of the

---

[5]Assembled and averaged from sources including Rosenstone and Wolfinger, in Niemi and Weisberg, eds., *Controversies in Voting Behavior.*

economy; for 18 percent, the vote seemed unrelated to any public issue.[6] Those who are unfamiliar with political issues are less likely to participate in politics.

Social and economic inequalities deprive many poor and minority citizens of cognitive and other skills that foster political participation. Even the white working class is affected to some extent. The more educated tend to have greater familiarity with political issues and participate most heavily, with college graduates voting at nearly twice the rate of those who did not complete high school.[7] Among school leavers, only half play active roles in organizations; four fifths of the college educated do so. More than three quarters of the lowest economic class belong to no organizations whatever, except perhaps to a church, whereas many upper-middle class people belong to numerous organizations.[8] Part of the difference is money, but the political psychology also is different:

> Upper class persons are those who are most likely to display those attitudes and personality traits that facilitate associational memberships. These include a sense of personal and political competence, achievement motivation, a distant time horizon, and a strong sense of duty.[9]

The difficulty this causes for policy making is illustrated by the experience of the National Welfare Rights Organization, which tried to construct a mass-based organization devoted to poor people's issues. Initiated by middle-class professional activists during the heyday of Lyndon Johnson's antipoverty programs, hundreds of local groups were organized. Thanks in part to membership benefits like grants for the purchase of furniture, some 22,000 members enrolled in the first three years. But most of these did not stick with it, and the local groups collapsed within a few years.[10] As a result, there is not much base for political mobilization when antipoverty programs come under attack.

Socialization

In large part, people participate in political life because socialized to do so. They learn from family, school, friends, clubs, and political parties the attitudes and dispositions to action which lead them to vote and otherwise

[6]Angus Campbell, Philip E. Converse, Warren E. Miller, and Donald E. Stokes, *The American Voter* (New York: John Wiley and Sons, Inc., 1960), p. 249.

[7]Frances Fox Piven and Richard Cloward, *Why Americans Don't Vote* (New York: Pantheon, 1987), p. 205.

[8]Herbert Hyman and Charles Wright, "Trends in Voluntary Association Membership of American Adults," *American Sociological Review* 36 (April 1971): 191–206.

[9]James Q. Wilson, *Political Organizations* (New York: Basic Books, 1973), p. 59.

[10]Frances Fox Piven and Richard A. Cloward, *Poor People's Movements* (New York: Pantheon, 1977). Also see Curt Lamb, *Political Power in Poor Neighborhoods* (New York: John Wiley & Sons, 1975).

participate. People participate if taught to believe it matters, if helped to acquire verbal and other skills of citizenship, if indoctrinated with aspirations and expectations that stimulate rather than paralyze, and if taught to see themselves as members of the political community. Citizens not socialized in these ways are not likely to vote or otherwise participate in politics. Even those who know which policies might serve their needs, and even those who have the motivation and energy to do something positive about their problems, may not see in voting or other participation any practical, realizable possibility of helping themselves. (This view may be as sensible as that of the activist citizen, considering the weakness of voting as a method of controlling public policy.)

Millions of nineteenth-century immigrants to the United States were crippled politically due to their socialization. Today the largest inactive groups are low-income minorities without the habits, aspirations, or expectations supporting participation. Their social isolation from politically active people impedes them from acquiring the most elementary necessary political information, skill, and hope.

Also contributing to political inequality is actual socialization *against* participation, toward withdrawal or nonparticipation. Many investigators have found evidence that public schools discourage participation through their emphasis on submission to authority, more for working-class children than upper-class children. The ways children are taught to think—and to not think—are discussed further in chapter 10.

Inequalities of information, education, and socialization converge. People differ greatly in their personal capacities to understand politics, in their belief that they can influence it, and in their effectiveness at it. For political influence, one needs time, knowledge of public affairs, a persuasive tongue or pen, status in the community, influential associates, and success in interpersonal relations. Millions of citizens have none of these skills, and therefore have great difficulty exerting influence in political life. They do not know how to play a useful organizational role, hardly dare to try, and are indifferently regarded by the actives in organizations. The highly educated, in contrast, find it easy to play some significant role in political organizations and are usually warmly welcomed to active membership. They can persuade, negotiate, analyze issues, raise money, organize events, or write position papers. They stand in sharp contrast to their more numerous fellow citizens. Contrast inhabitants of the Bronx with a graduating class at Harvard or Stanford in terms of preparedness for political participation.

ORGANIZATION, FUNDING, AND ACCESS

Beyond voting and attempting to persuade friends and neighbors, participation in choosing and influencing public officials requires an organization. Alone, the ordinary citizen can do almost nothing, even if he or she has the information and talent to do so. People must join together with others through interest groups or campaign organizations by giving them time, skill, or money.

Organizations and candidates need to pay newspapers, broadcasting stations, and their own office staffs and to engage speech writers, television producers, "advance men," lobbyists, publicists, and a long list of others. They also need money for typewriters, copy machines, postage, telephones—all the elementary tools of politics. A congressman makes the point through overstatement: "We deal in two things here—votes and the money used to persuade votes."[11] Unusually affluent individuals can contribute to political organizations more than the entire income of many poorer citizens. At an extreme, Ross Perot was said to have allocated up to $100 million of his own funds for his 1992 presidential campaign, a sum that would be difficult to raise from millions of average to low-income persons.[12]

Despite their great numbers, the poor can afford only a few, relatively impoverished political organizations, while the well-off have a much wider variety of well-financed endeavors. This is not simply an inequality between the very affluent and the poor, however, for inequality in organizations runs through the whole society. Union members mobilize far less money for political organizations than do businesspeople in most nations; and nonunion labor, accounting for over half of American workers not in professional or managerial positions, has essentially no organized access to funds and therefore goes largely unrepresented.[13]

In some European nations, a majority of employees are represented by strong labor unions and by political parties attuned to workers' issues. Moreover, taxation and social welfare systems greatly reduce economic disparities. These factors substantially narrow, but do not eliminate, the translation of economic inequalities into political ones.

Wealth, Favors, and Deference

Funding thus is a fundamental source of inequality in democratic policy making. The influence of wealth runs through many channels, from the financing of persuasion via contributions to campaign expenses to explicit buying of political favors. The line between legal and illegal channels blurs when a donor disguises a bribe as a contribution to a candidate's campaign. Many people know that there is an old tradition in American politics that a very large contribution can buy an ambassadorial appointment. Less conspicuously

---

[11]"Business Lobbying," *Consumer Reports* 43 (September 1978): 529.

[12]On campaign financing more generally, see Frank J. Sorauf, *Inside Campaign Finance: Myths and Realities* (New Haven, CT: Yale University Press, 1992).

[13]On organizational resources of interest groups, see Kay Lehman Schlozman and John T. Tierney, *Organized Interests and American Democracy* (New York: Harper & Row, 1986).

and with an unknown frequency, contributions and other favors can buy desired legislative votes or administrative rulings.

The Keating Five, senators who intervened with bank regulators on behalf of a wealthy savings and loan owner, illustrate a tendency that usually is conducted in less blatant fashion. As an aide to the donor said later, "Senators are extremely busy people. The donations were a way of getting their attention for our problem." In this case, both the wealthy donor and the elected officials were considered to have stepped over the line of legitimate behavior, but the point here is that donations are a normal part of the process by which busy officials set priorities for their time, and most citizens are excluded from the bidding due to lack of capital.

More generally, many people habitually defer to the wealthy and confer authority on them, in part due to the prospect of favors the wealthy can offer to those about them. Some legislators, for example, find it difficult to refuse free airplane trips, the loan of automobiles, and the pleasures of dinner parties and weekends with the wealthy. Even if under these circumstances the legal and informal rules of politics succeed in prohibiting an explicit exchange of favor for favor, many elected functionaries nevertheless will feel a solicitous concern for wealthy acquaintances and may tilt tax or other policy making toward actions the wealthy would favor.

In a technological society in which great wealth is based on business rather than on land, the elite of wealth tends to merge with the elite of business. Both accrue advantages in policy making from what they can offer to induce people to do as they wish.

INEQUALITY AND INTELLIGENT POLICY MAKING

Political inequality obviously reduces the extent to which policy making can be fully democratic. Not quite so apparent is that inequality interferes also with the *intelligence* of democracy.

If government functionaries are to focus their attention on important social problems, the broader policy-making process needs to help them see and conceptualize those problems. Since "importance" is partly in the eye of the beholder, governmental priority setting will be a weighted average of many people's judgments about which problems are most pressing. If poorer, less educated minorities participate less, their judgments about which problems deserve government's attention will attain less than proportionate weight in the process of partisan mutual adjustment. Just as importantly, when some important problems are not forcefully called to attention, then all of us are deprived of the opportunity to deliberate about them, deprived of the opportunity to reappraise our own judgments of what issues most deserve scarce time, attention, and funding.

Thus, hunger in America is periodically "discovered" instead of remaining high on the agenda until it is taken care of. This occurs in part because the hungry lack the skills, organization, funding, and energy to press their cause effectively. Likewise, homelessness was discovered as a national policy problem long after it actually grew to serious proportions. The problems of young blacks remain low on governmental agendas even though one quarter of black males under age 30 spend time in jail, and several million young black women face staggering obstacles trying to rear their children in low-income, single-parent households.

Once an issue has been taken onto government's agenda, inequality can affect how a social problem comes to be defined. Established social welfare bureaucracies, affluent legislators, and the business community tend to define homelessness, hunger, and crime quite differently than those with more direct experience of these problems. For example, all of these issues could be seen as symptoms of a single underlying problem: a skewed distribution of income and wealth. There is no single, "correct" way to define complex problems, of course, and it is sensible for numerous partially competing explanations and definitions to be promulgated—as indeed they are. To the extent, however, that political influence is unequally distributed, some people's definitions will have a lot higher probability of being accepted than others. And inequalities in problem definition grade immediately into unequal influence in negotiating proposed solutions.

Finally, political inequality renders almost impossible one of the key tasks that a successful government would need to achieve: alleviating unjustified inequalities produced by economic life. The undeniable merits of using markets as a mechanism for carrying out many public tasks, discussed in chapter 1, do not negate the fact that market systems distribute income and wealth grossly unequally. There is wide agreement that sensible social policy requires government to redress the imbalance regarding who shall have how much. What a fairer and otherwise more sensible distribution of income and wealth would look like is open to all parties for inquiry, debate, and judgment. Political judgments, differing in various nations and changing over time, determine tax rates for rich and poor, old age pensions, eligibility for food stamps, minimum wage laws, and other welfare state policies.

While the affluent and the middle classes obviously have worthwhile and significant views to contribute to the ongoing debates and reappraisals, the disadvantaged themselves know a great deal about some of these problems. Their welfare rights organizations, as well as many scholars who study governmental programs serving low-income clients, routinely point out the ways that poor people's problems come to be defined in middle-class bureaucrats' terms. Yet poor people's shortage of political skill, finance, and participation means that their voices may be barely heard. Thus, not only do the poor lack the buying power to exert much influence as consumers in retail markets; and not only do they lack the skills to exert much leverage as workers in labor markets; but the very people who fare worst in economic life also are least able to be effective in political life. One inequality is heaped on another. A personal tragedy for those who suffer this fate, it also is a significant blow to the efficacy of social problem solving.

Chapter 10

Impaired Inquiry

Because democratic political interaction is the primary basis for wise policy making, the quality of people's thinking can have a huge influence on whether their interactions result in sensible and fair policy agreements. Extended inquiry into the thinking abilities and inquiry skills of both ordinary citizens and political elites therefore may be among the most consequential investigations students of public policy can make in trying to understand what goes right and wrong in the effort to shape society.[1]

In some respects, the populations of affluent societies seem better prepared than ever before for thoughtful reflection concerning political issues. The percentage of voters who are college graduates is at a historic high; television brings analysis of national and global events into our living rooms; children are less dominated by parents than in some earlier periods; and many people now take more skeptical attitudes toward government, business, and other social institutions than they did a generation or two ago.

Still, few of us come close to the capacities for inquiry and understanding that some democratic theorists have assumed—and that we all might wish. Our

---

[1]This chapter is drawn largely from Charles E. Lindblom, *Inquiry and Change: The Troubled Attempt to Understand and Shape Society* (New Haven, CT: Yale University Press, 1990), especially chapters 5–8.

incapacities derive in part from biological limitations: We cannot simultaneously consider more than a few angles on a problem; perceptions and interpretations become distorted in systematic ways, as in our tendency to recall vivid events and forget others; and our memories are weak compared with those of a computer.[2] On top of these and other biological limitations, there is a huge category of socially caused or exacerbated impairments.

Cognitive psychologists find that most of us have great difficulty making logical inferences, either on personal or social issues.[3] We easily form emotional attachments or antipathies to political abstractions, like "capitalism" or "the Soviet Union," and thereby become vulnerable to simplistic thinking and symbolic manipulation.[4] We tend to retreat from complex issues into apathy, acquiring only "inches of facts" about political life instead of the yards or miles actually required to make sense of contemporary issues.[5]

Impaired thinking reduces the intelligence of policy making because each individual is less capable of playing his or her role in partisan interaction. Policy making also becomes less democratic, because impaired thinking makes it easier for elites to preserve their advantages. Consider the evidence.

SCHOOLING AND OTHER SOURCES OF IMPAIRMENT

Research in many nations has documented the extent to which education, the very institution on which we rely most heavily for helping children learn inquiry and thinking skills, has been conceived and used as an instrument to control the masses.[6] As if responding to Adam Smith's early concerns about education leading to "disorder," educational policy has attempted to construct schooling to induce habits of compliance at the expense of children's development of skills useful for thoughtful dissent and inquiry. Contemporary business leaders, teachers, and government officials proclaim it "our highest duty to pronounce enthusiastically, and with unanimous voice, for the supremacy of law and the

---

[2]Daniel Kahneman, Paul Slovic, and Amos Tversky, *Judgment Under Uncertainty: Heuristics and Biases* (New York: Cambridge University Press, 1982).

[3]Richard E. Nisbet and Lee Ross, *Human Inference* (Englewood Cliffs, NJ: Prentice Hall, 1980).

[4]Henry Brady and Paul Sniderman, "Attitude Attribution," *American Political Science Review* 79 (December 1985). On symbolic politics, see Murray Edelman, *The Symbolic Uses of Politics* (Urbana, IL: University of Illinois Press, 1985).

[5]Aaron Wildavsky, "Choosing Preferences by Constructing Institutions: A Cultural Theory of Preference Formation," *American Political Science Review* 81 (March 1987): 3–21, quote from p. 8.

[6]See, among many other examples, Ira Katznelson and Margaret Wier, *Schooling for All* (New York: Basic Books, 1985); Mary Jo Maynes, *Schooling in Western Europe* (Albany: State University of New York Press, 1985); and Nubuo Shimahara, *Adaptation and Education in Japan* (New York: Praeger, 1979).

maintenance of social and political order.''[7] Employers in particular have sought from schooling a docile workforce accustomed to following assignments with little question and to accepting the existing social, economic, and political order.[8]

Most of us want order, of course. The problem arises when it becomes a dogma and interferes with children learning to think, question, and negotiate. As found in a study of 12,000 schoolchildren,

> Compliance to rules and authority is the major focus of civics education in elementary schools. The three items rated as more important than basic subjects (reading and arithmetic) by a majority of second- and third-grade teachers were the law, the policeman, and the child's obligation to conform to school rules and laws of the community.[9]

Schools discriminate by socioeconomic class, generally preparing lower-status students for even less thoughtful lives than the relatively impaired and indoctrinated middle- to upper-status students.[10]

Studies of French secondary education compare pupils there with bureaucrats and assembly-line workers, and speak of "traditionally designed textbooks that are dogmatic in style."[11] A United Nations study of twenty-one countries found that schools tend to make "people easy to govern" and to "cultivate unthinking respect for hierarchies."[12] Even in the 1990s, after there has been ample time for the social criticisms of the previous decades to seep into curricula throughout the world, existing political-economic institutions generally still are applauded rather than probed.

Parents

Parents are themselves impaired probers, scarred by schooling and other social forces. In turn, a great many parents teach their children not to be very reflective about much of life. Starting from infancy, most caregivers tell their

---

[7]David B. Tyack, *The One Best System* (Cambridge, MA: Harvard University Press, 1974), p. 74.

[8]Herbert G. Gutman, "Work, Culture and Society in Industrializing America, 1815–1919," *American Historical Review* 78 (June 1973); and Samuel Bowles and Herbert Gintis, *Schooling in Capitalist America* (New York: Basic Books, 1976), argue that business elites have exerted primary influence; interpretations suggesting control by several interacting elites are offered by Katznelson and Weir, *Schooling for All*, and by Brian Simon, *The Politics of Educational Reform, 1920–1940* (London: Lawrence and Wishart, 1974).

[9]Robert D. Hess and Judith V. Torney, *The Development of Political Attitudes in Children* (Chicago: Aldine, 1967), p. 110.

[10]James Rosenbaum, *Making Inequality* (New York: John Wiley & Sons, 1976); Caroline Hodges Persell, *Education and Inequality* (New York: Free Press, 1977), chapter 7.

[11]William Schonfield, *Obedience and Revolt* (Beverly Hills: Sage, 1976); W.R. Fraser, *Reforms and Restraints in Modern French Education* (London: Routledge & Kegan Paul, 1971), p. 143.

[12]International Commission on the Development of Education, *Learning to Be* (Paris: Unesco, 1972), pp. 58, 64.

children "no" many dozen times during the course of a day. A few of those episodes concern undeniable, serious dangers like fire or automobiles; most, however, are more for the parent's convenience than because the child's exploration actually threatens his or her well-being.

Slightly more subtle are parental inculcations not to fuss, not to talk back to adults, and to obey. Superficially, these typical parental behaviors do not appear alarming, since children need to develop socially acceptable ways of behaving. But there is a large body of research suggesting that even minor forms of indoctrination and command, repeated often and strongly enough, can help imprison the mind and create lasting habits of subservience.[13]

Working-class parents seem to be even more likely than middle-class parents to opt for power-oriented childrearing. "They are less likely to give reasons for their commands or to encourage the child to make his own decisions in family matters. They appear to be less concerned with the child's opinion and to give him fewer alternatives for action or for thought."[14] Lower levels of verbal skill coupled with jobs where there is not much room for self-direction appear to account for part of the differences in childrearing techniques among classes.[15]

Peer Groups and Media

Beyond particular interactions with parental and educational authority figures, children and adults alike are subjected to impairing influences during much of their waking lives. All of us interact with peers in ways that extend and concentrate impairments; indeed, the term peer group appropriately evokes an image of unthinking conformity to group standards of behavior. Even with their comparative freedom from economic responsibilities, only a minority of teenagers identify with subcultures and local peer groups actively challenging the dominant culture's values. No peer group encourages intense probing and disagreement regarding its own norms, not even university professors.

The media likewise tend to constrain more than to promote probing. News reporting sometimes is said to be "objective," simply informing the reader or viewer. But, as everyone knows, mainstream print and broadcast news offers thoroughly conventional interpretations of current events; so their effect is to reiterate and strengthen a society's dominant views more than to challenge and probe. Even when conflicting interpretations are offered, these almost always fall within a narrow range, with political and economic interpretations diverging far less than those concerning music, lifestyles, fashion, and the arts. The more politically dissenting a group, the less favorable is the treatment accorded it, and

---

[13]For a review, see Viktor Gecas, "Contexts of Socialization," in Morris Rosenberg and Ralph H. Turner, eds., *Social Psychology* (New York: Basic Books, 1981) pp. 164–99.

[14]Hess and Torney, *Development of Political Attitudes*, p. 126.

[15]Gecas, "Contexts of Socialization"; Melvin L. Kohn, *Class and Conformity* (Homewood, IL: Dorsey Press, 1969).

the less coverage it receives (except for dramatic disturbances like strikes and riots).[16] Even labor unions have difficulty getting media coverage in the United States.

Do media stories really influence people? Media scholars have compiled massive documentation showing "the power of the media to say what is politically real and legitimate and what is not; to establish certain political agendas for social attention and to contain, channel, and exclude others."[17] The media are "stunningly successful" in telling people what to think about and what to not think about.[18] This is not to say that journalists are advocates; Dan Rather, Peter Jennings, and Tom Brokaw obviously do not take overt stands on the issues of the day, and professional standards rule out deliberate, gross distortions. But "balanced" and "nonpartisan" messages tend to converge around the society's modal opinions, so media "impartiality" really implies a certain conformity to dominant opinions. As discussed throughout this and previous chapters, dominant opinions advantage elites; so business as usual in the media reinforces historically inherited patterns of elite advantages.

Unilateral Communications from Elite to Mass

Implicit in the foregoing discussion is that virtually all public communication goes from elite to mass: Campaign speeches, advertisements, opinion columns in newspapers, television programming, and pronouncements from government officials typically originate with members of the advantaged segments of the population. This seems so natural that one is hard-pressed to imagine how it could be otherwise. But the result is that elites urge their messages on ordinary people more or less unilaterally, instead of having to engage in a somewhat equal interchange.

The democracies do not have elite dominance in communication like that found in earlier fascist and communist systems, of course, where mass media conveyed whatever government officials wanted. But the technologies of electronic media have greatly expanded the capacity of elites to reach mass audiences. Misrepresentation, deceit, and obfuscation now can be disseminated on a vast scale, as in touting high-technology weaponry during the Gulf War and proclaiming it a great victory, when in fact subsequent studies have raised serious doubts about both the war's achievements and about the performance of the Stealth fighter and Scud missile.

---

[16]Pamela J. Shoemaker, "Media Treatment of Deviant Political Groups," *Journalism Quarterly* 61 (Spring 1984): 66–75, 82; and Terence H. Qualter, *Opinion Control in the Democracies* (London: Macmillan, 1985), p. 198.

[17]Todd Gitlin, "Media Sociology," *Theory and Society* 6 (September 1978): 205.

[18]Shanto Iyengar and Donald R. Kinder, *News That Matters* (Chicago: University of Chicago Press, 1988).

"Free speech" as conventionally understood clearly does not ensure a real competition of ideas, because access to mass communication is extremely costly and only those with the capital have real access.[19] Speeches and public relations efforts by business executives usually endorse the political and economic status quo—including employer dominance over workers and the necessity of great economic inequalities. They extol democracy in its present form—implicitly opposing further democratic innovations—and they routinely argue that government is encroaching excessively on business, to the detriment of the public.[20] In advertising, of course, most communications are designed to *prevent* the viewer, reader, or listener from carefully probing the merits of a product. And public affairs communications by business often are designed to "sow the seeds of confusion."[21]

Political rhetoric likewise seems intended "not to persuade, but to control; not to stimulate thought, but to prevent it; not to convey information, but to conceal or distort it; not to draw public attention, but to divert or suppress it."[22] Everyone knows that campaign speeches and ads intentionally misrepresent and oversimplify; but so do ordinary speeches by presidents and prime ministers, as well as congressional newsletters and political party communications. Political elites inundate citizens with messages designed to shape and inhibit their demands without losing their support.

The media serve elites not because of any conspiracy, but for perfectly mundane reasons. Most importantly, in an inegalitarian society it seems entirely natural to journalists and their audiences that stories should be based largely on what elites are doing and saying. The nature of the journalism business also imposes a gentle tyranny known as the deadline. Government elites hold news conferences, pass out news releases, issue reports—all easy to cover in the morning edition or the 6:00 P.M. broadcast. Journalists rarely can afford the time and expense of extended research, as in trying to figure out how to make a story out of chronic persistent hunger in central Africa. Even when there is a catastrophic famine that has to be covered, those interviewed typically are government officials, not political dissenters calling for radical economic and political changes on grounds that the existing system clearly has failed. The effect of continual quoting of persons in positions of authority is that their opinions often come to circulate as fact.

[19]Benjamin Ginsberg, *The Captive Public* (New York: Basic Books, 1986).

[20]See, for example, Sidney Verba and Gary R. Orren, *Equality in America: The View From the Top* (Cambridge, MA: Harvard University Press, 1985).

[21]Thomas Milan Konda, "Political Advertising and Public Relations by Business in the United States," Ph.D. dissertation (Department of Political Science, University of Kentucky, 1983), p. 32.

[22]Paul E. Corcoran, *Political Language and Rhetoric* (St. Lucia, Queensland: University of Queensland Press, 1979), p. 175.

Results of Impairment

Every culture's beliefs, values, and actions have been molded through processes such as those discussed above. As anthropologist Ruth Benedict observed regarding traditional cultures,

> The life-history of the individual is first and foremost an accommodation to the patterns and standards traditionally handed down in his community. From the moment of his birth, the customs into which he is born shape his experience and behavior. By the time he can talk, he is the little creature of his culture, and by the time he is grown and able to take part in its activities, its habits are his habits, its beliefs are his beliefs, its impossibilities his impossibilities.[23]

Some of this socialization is necessary for society to be viable, exactly how much no one knows. And some of it is helpful to the individual's inquiry efforts. But the majority of socializing influences encourage like-mindedness, "censorship and deception that in turn promote ignorance."[24]

Some ideas thereby come close to silencing others, excluding them from discussion as irrelevant, inappropriate, or even unthinkable. This may not be a problem in traditional cultures; in technological societies, however, excessive conformity fundamentally undermines social problem solving. It stifles the competition of ideas on which successful democratic political interaction depends. Conformity rules out policy options that could be quite useful in attacking a problem. And policy trials tend to rigidify because of inadequate scrutiny, lack of creative reflection, and too little openness to new ideas; this frustrates the trial-and-error process that underlies sensible human decision making.

IMPAIRMENT AND ELITE ADVANTAGE

In addition to generally degrading the quality of policy making, one particular consequence of impaired probing is that economic and political elites have an easier time preserving their advantages.

Suspiciously High Levels of Agreement

Considering the limitations of analysis, the complexity of public policy issues, and the myriad opportunities for people's interests to be in conflict, one might expect to find people disagreeing fundamentally with each other over virtually everything. Instead, politics normally proceeds on the basis of what some call the "underlying consensus" in a society. Is this agreement brought about

---

[23]Ruth Benedict, *Patterns of Culture* (Boston: Houghton Mifflin, 1961), p. 2.
[24]Larry Spence, *The Politics of Social Knowledge* (University Park: Pennsylvania State University Press, 1984), p. 60.

mainly via reasoned persuasion, or does much of it evolve through the social in-doctrination processes previously discussed? Who has the capacity and incentive to use schooling and other socializing institutions to bring about widespread agreements?

When universal male suffrage was granted in England, Karl Marx predicted that the masses of working people would use their votes to dismantle the structure of wealth and privilege under which they suffered great deprivation. That they did not do so, that no body of citizens in any democracy has done so, represents an extraordinary fact. Throughout the world a large majority refrains from trying to use government to assault the privileges of the most favored strata or classes in society, including ownership of wealth itself. Somehow people have learned not to attack what looks like an irresistible target.

This is true despite massive evidence that the economic system awards large sums to some people who do not play a socially productive role (junk bond sales-people), while awarding next to nothing to some who play socially crucial roles (preschool teachers). Opinions about redistribution of income and wealth differ somewhat among nations, but there is substantial agreement in most wealthy countries to leave this largely up to market forces. People disagree on many connected secondary issues, of course, such as on exact types and rates of taxation. But the agreement on basic structural features seems solid.

More generally, people display widespread agreement on the structure of their society and on the rules of the political process. Despite marked distaste for budgetary and other stalemates among the House, Senate, and President, Americans overwhelmingly agree on maintaining the present Constitution with its checks and balances that arguably cripple American government and prevent effective policy making. Americans also largely agree on maintaining private enterprise in more or less its present form, opposing European-style laws that mandate lengthy paid vacations, advance notification and workforce retraining when a major business is closing a plant, and worker participation in decision making.

Indoctrination, Obfuscation, Suppression

Who or what has taught hundreds of millions of people to refrain from challenging the fundamentals of existing political and economic processes? Some observers believe that ordinary people understand the need for an elite. Even it were true that the great mass of voters benefited from an elite of wealth and privilege (for purposes of argument one can grant the possibility), it is inconceivable that voters in all the democracies, historical and contemporary, could *know* this to be true. Indeed, social scientists do not know it to be true or false; there are plausible arguments, pro and con. So if voters everywhere have believed in perpetuating great inequality, their agreement must be explained by some social process that has induced, channeled, and forced widespread alignment—not by people's shared insight into reasonably well proven fact.

That no democracy has put on its agenda a major frontal assault on wealth and its attendant privileges is a historical fact of pivotal importance, for in an open-minded exploration of possible policies concerning the wealthy, the probability that some democracy would attempt such an attack is extremely high. Some democratic governments—Sweden, for example—have pushed modest attacks on inequality, but even the progressive forces there never actually pushed for full political and economic equality.[25] Some European socialist parties have declared their intention to do so, to mount a major assault on inequality; but on winning power they have not in fact followed through. This approaches zero probability, except on the assumption of a powerful uniform social indoctrination, coupled with vigorous efforts to choke off a genuine competition of ideas.

The same can be said of the relatively passive acceptance of present ways of structuring large corporations and the market economy. This economic system is prone to recession and depression, environmental destruction in pursuit of profit, and massive dislocation of families and whole communities as factories move overseas, go bankrupt, or fall victim to corporate merger. Informed intellectuals argue over the feasibility of alternative ways of organizing economic life; so it is not the case that everyone knows the alternatives cannot work. Again, therefore, the uniform rejection of major change by all democracies seems to require explanation.

It is not surprising that those people most favored by an existing social system will wish to "teach its virtues" to those not favored. History records many successful attempts, such as the medieval doctrine that heavenly pleasures await those who do not challenge the dominant earthly order. In our era, elites of wealth and business wish to persuade the citizenry to accept a concentration of wealth and its attendant privileges, corporate autonomy, and the privileged position of business—all as necessary to the citizen's welfare.

Earlier chapters have already provided the evidence of elites' capacities for engaging in persuasive efforts. The "competition of ideas" that ostensibly characterizes a democracy is an unequal competition, with political persuasion enormously one-sided. For all the reasons given in the discussions of business privilege, interest groups, and inequality, dissident voices cannot speak as loudly or as frequently as the voices of wealth and business, especially on those issues on which government officials join with business.

Neither the wealthy nor business leadership constitutes a wholly homogeneous opinion group, of course; elites disagree on countless issues, and citizens benefit from debate and conflict among them.[26] But these disagreements are about secondary issues, such as whether new automobiles will have to achieve

---

[25]Sidney Verba, et al., *Elites and the Idea of Equality: A Comparison of Japan, Sweden, and the United States* (Cambridge, MA: Harvard University Press, 1987), chapter 7.

[26]For detailed evidence on the point, see David Vogel, *Fluctuating Fortunes: The Political Power of Business in America* (New York: Basic Books, 1989).

27.5 or 40 miles per gallon, not about challenges to basic aspects of the political and economic systems. On primary issues there is much greater agreement among government functionaries, business executives, and other elites, and they carry virtually the same message to citizens, indoctrinating them in regard to these issues, making democratic control circular or short-circuited.[27]

This high degree of homogeneity on primary issues means that some possible alternative policies never appear on the policy-making agenda. Political elites neither debate nor propose action, for example, on replacing the president with a prime minister. Bureaucratic and judicial processes to establish and implement environmental regulations are tortuously slow and frequently ineffectual; yet environmental groups rarely press for simpler and more effective methods, such as sending business executives to jail for violating pollution limits. It is not necessary to endorse any particular policy moves to see that mainstream debate fails to examine numerous options for handling serious political problems. A large set of plausible options somehow is being kept off the political agenda.

To illustrate further the narrowness of contemporary debates, consider the general problem of bending business to public purposes while retaining the incentives and other virtues of market-oriented, competitive businesses. It is hard to miss the possibility of maintaining present arrangements concerning private ownership, competition, and so forth but enacting laws to make chief executive officers of large corporations much more accountable for those aspects of their policy making that have substantial public consequences. Civil and criminal penalties could be toughened as well as extended to a broader range of behaviors—such as pollution, failing to compete effectively with foreign industry, or providing shoddy products. Or, more positively, lucrative government-funded bonuses could be paid to CEOs who achieve great gains in these areas. Alternatively, or in addition, top business executives could be made subject to removal by presidents or prime ministers.

These and other similar policies are easy to imagine and much more powerful than the timid incentives and sanctions that governments now employ to induce prosocial behavior from businesses. So it is astounding not to find such proposals on the political agenda for active consideration. No one knows what the effects would be, of course; so any actual implementation of the proposals would need to be gradual and experimental. And, on further inspection, these policy proposals might be shelved in favor of other ways of trying to achieve the same general goal. But that the matter is not even being carefully studied and debated is strong evidence that hundreds of millions of people are not using their wits.

Thus, non-elites lack capacities for thinking clearly about the ways they are disadvantaged by society's present status hierarchies, income and wealth dis-

---

[27]On circularity in economic and political decision making, see Charles E. Lindblom, *Politics and Markets: The World's Political-Economic Systems* (New York: Basic Books, 1977).

tributions, and political-economic institutions. Impairments help prevent ordinary people from gaining the skills and open-mindedness to inquire into the sources of their disadvantages, or to explore policy options that might ameliorate present inequities. People may actually come to *believe* that systematic and enduring patterns of disadvantages are deserved and even desirable.[28] Thus in a grossly unequal competition of ideas, the advantages of the wealthy and of business strike at the very foundation of democracy—the capacity of the citizen to analyze his or her own needs and to find policies for meeting them.

CONCLUSION

The conclusion of this chapter can be set alongside earlier conclusions about the looseness of popular control in contemporary democratic systems. On the usual issues of politics, many obstacles impede effective citizen control over policy making, obstacles identified chapter by chapter. Only on a few issues that we call primary, such as leaving income distribution largely up to market forces, do governments consistently give citizens what they say they want. On these primary issues, however, citizens appear to be partially indoctrinated to ask mainly for what elites already wish to give them. On the primary issues, popular control therefore becomes to some significant degree circular. An indoctrinated citizenry does not put potentially troublesome proposals for fundamental change on the agenda. Even speculation on radical new forms of social organization is left to a relative handful of poets, professors, utopian novelists, musicians, and writers of comic strips.

On reflection, few thoughtful people are likely to disagree that human inquiry is seriously flawed. And in certain respects it is entirely obvious that the quality of humanity's capacity for probing individual, organizational, and collective problems lies at the heart of social problem solving. Hence, even those who remain unconvinced by the argument regarding elite advantage may be able to agree on the desirability of placing reduction of impairment much higher on our individual and collective agendas.

Since both inquiry skills and impairments are socially taught and learned in large part, over an extended period it may prove possible to shift the balance toward skill and away from impairment. If families, schools, and work organizations are an important source of impaired intelligence, however, then improvements in individual and collective capacities for thinking about problems presumably would require changes in these fundamental institutions. How that task might be pursued in concert with other tasks emerging from this analysis is the subject of the remaining chapters.

---

[28]Jennifer L. Hochschild, *What's Fair? American Beliefs about Distributive Justice* (Cambridge, MA: Harvard University Press, 1981).

PART IV

IMPROVING POLICY MAKING

Chapter 11

Making the Most of Analysis

The obstacles to social problem solving reviewed in earlier chapters are formidable. People are limited and impaired in their capacities for probing social problems and policy options. Inequalities are rampant, with the advantages held by business and the wealthy combining to virtually rule out a wide range of policy options that would challenge key elements of the status quo. Political institutions are not well designed for social problem solving. Given all this, is there any realistic prospect of doing significantly better at steering society?

Perhaps not. But changes do occur decade by decade that initially seem highly improbable—civil rights in the 1960s, environmental protection legislation in the 1970s, and the demise of communism in the 1980s. No one knows exactly how best to build on this political progress, but one key to it surely would need to be changes in people's *ideas*—about social problems, about policy possibilities, and about policy processes and institutions.

Unfortunately for deliberate efforts to accelerate political progress, it is far from obvious how to get more people to have better ideas. Nor can we expect agreement on what the better ideas are—that is a matter for partisan dispute. But most people who believe in democracy, on reflection, may be able to agree that a strengthened competition of ideas is a core element in improving the capacity for intelligent, democratic policy making. Chapter 12 explores the desirability and feasibility of unleashing the powers of ordinary people to probe social problems much more skillfully and assertively than they now do, in part by seeking to reduce the extent of business privilege, inequality, and impaired thinking.

This chapter takes up a much narrower, but closely related task: the possible contribution of professional policy analysts to an invigorated competition of ideas. There is no cookbook formula for this. But one prerequisite is to get beyond the conventional view of policy analysis, the familiar but naive notion that the analyst's job is to provide government officials with nonpartisan, comprehensive solutions for social problems. The role and task of analysis are not nearly that simple, as should be apparent by now.

Among other changes necessary to make the most of analysis, we examine three. To be more usable, analysis first needs to better adapt to the partisan nature of political life: How can analysts best serve to make partisan interactions more thoughtful and effective? Second, analysis needs to better adjust to the fact that social problem solving requires coping with uncertainty and value conflicts in a context of inadequate time, attention, and resources: What strategies can we offer for coping *better*? Third, certain professional impairments detract from policy professionals' thoughtful probing of human problems and possibilities: Which impairments need what sort of reconsideration and reduction?

ADAPTING ANALYSIS TO POLITICS

Policy analysts and scholars recognize that uncertainty and disagreement seldom can be avoided in any realm of political life, because there are compelling reasons for them (see chapter 2). Nevertheless, neither textbook treatments of policy problems, nor governmental analyses such as those by the General Accounting Office, nor independent scholars' policy thinking is explicitly and systematically adapted to being useful in settings characterized by high uncertainty, partisan disagreement, and interactive problem solving. Policy discussions typically slip into behaving as if uncertainty and disagreement could be circumvented by sufficient information or logic.[1] One of the crucial steps in improving policy analysis, therefore, is to adapt it better to the inevitability and the desirability of partisan conflict as the key mechanism in the intelligence of democracy. In other words, analysis should aim to improve the quality of political interaction, not try to substitute for it.

Those engaged in policy disputes routinely seek to buttress their argu-

---

[1] The epitome of the uncertainty- and disagreement-denying textbook is Edith Stokey and Richard Zeckhauser, *A Primer for Policy Analysis* (New York: W. W. Norton, 1978). But even some otherwise excellent texts do not succeed entirely in adapting their analytic methods to a partisan context; see, for example, Garry D. Brewer and Peter deLeon, *The Foundations of Policy Analysis* (Homewood, IL: Dorsey, 1983).

ments via analysis, of course. Thus, over a period of years the EPA offered more than a dozen technical claims regarding the need to take lead out of gasoline; every one of the claims was plausibly rebutted by Ethyl Corporation, the major manufacturer of lead additives for gasoline.[2] Legislators frequently are presented with such conflicting, analysis-based claims, leading one frustrated senator to exclaim, "I wish at some time somebody would . . . tell the committee categorically a nuclear reactor is safe or isn't safe, so that the public will know exactly where it stands."[3]

To the contrary, government functionaries almost always are left making judgments in the face of uncertainty. Analysts sometimes can narrow the range of legitimate disagreement, but not enough to obviate the need for political judgments. A majority of atmospheric scientists, for example, believe there will be climate warming from combustion of fossil fuels and release of other greenhouse gases. But they disagree markedly regarding how much warming, how soon, and what should be done about it.[4] Enormous room for interpretation likewise characterizes disputes over policy for education, crime, and other social issues.

Partisan Analysis

Is analysis futile, then, because it normally is inconclusive? Perhaps so under the conventional view that policy professionals are supposed to provide neutral "answers" to some public official with comprehensive responsibilities in a problem area. Recognizing, however, that government functionaries and other political participants deal at any given time with limited problems, within limited perspectives, and have to make due with limited analytical capacities, new possibilities are opened.

Analysis for Conflict Resolution

Whenever two or more political participants think about a policy problem, there is a good chance they will come up with different ideas regarding what, if anything, should be done. Hence, they face a task of conflict resolution, which can be accomplished through some mix of three methods:

1. Nonrational and irrational persuasion, as via propaganda campaigns or symbolic rhetoric;

[2]David Collingridge and Colin Reeve, *Science Speaks to Power: The Role of Experts in Policy Making* (New York: St. Martin's Press, 1986), p. 44.

[3]Senator John O. Pastore, in U.S. Congress, Joint Committee on Atomic Energy, hearings on "The Status of Nuclear Reactor Safety," 1973.

[4]Contrast the call to arms offered by Stephen H. Schneider, *Global Warming: Are We Entering the Greenhouse Century?* (New York: Random House, 1990) with the moderate depiction by John Firor, *The Changing Atmosphere: A Global Challenge* (New Haven, CT: Yale University Press, 1990) and William R. Cline, *Economics of Global Warming* (Washington, DC: Institute for International Economics, 1992).

2. Logrolling, vetoes, bribery, or other interpersonal means for inducing acquiescence without actually persuading on the merits; and
3. Informed and reasoned persuasion.

For raising the level of intelligence in policy making, it clearly is the last of these methods that is required.

What role can analysis play in promoting reasoned persuasion as a means of conflict resolution? To begin with, some participants in policy making could look for aspects of a problem that, if brought to light, might reduce conflict and lead toward agreement. For example, proponents of a school voucher plan may be able to come up with a mechanism for making the proposal less threatening to teachers' unions. Analysis thereby can serve as an instrument of persuasion—of persuasion in the best sense of the word, meaning the use of information and thought to move people closer to reasoned and voluntary agreement. This is achieved in part by persuading possible opponents that their views are being taken into account—a use of analysis that does not require conclusiveness, only plausibility.

Analysis that seeks reasoned persuasion regarding particular aspects of an issue can often be effective where more ambitious forms of analysis cannot. Although useful analysis of a vast problem typically cannot be completed, especially within the time and resources available, more modest analysis can be very helpful in the task of persuasion.

When the Office of Management and Budget or an appropriations subcommittee in Congress scrutinizes agency budgets, attempting to reconcile huge budget aspirations with limited resources, analysis plays an important but modest role. Rather than attempting to "understand" the budget as a whole, and rather than looking at budget expansions and contractions in the abstract, participants instead focus their energies on finding out what budgetary changes might be able to win agreement. They exchange proposals and supporting information for why certain programs should be cut or should be exempt from cuts. Analysis can play a key role in this process. For example, in trying to put caps on Medicare or other entitlement expenditures, fiscal conservatives may gather data on a few key trends, hoping to convince even the fiscal liberals that expenditures are growing exponentially and that some systematic intervention is necessary. This makes the analytic task far more manageable in three ways: (1) Partisans focus scarce analytic resources on policy *proposals,* rather than on the budget more generically; (2) they concentrate on proposals that stand some chance of winning agreement; and (3) analysis focuses especially on those proposals that seem unlikely to succeed without additional information useful in the task of reasoned persuasion.

Thoughtful Partisanship?

If analysis is used by particular partisans interacting with each other—not by "society" more generally, and not by a mastermind with an olympian view of public policy—one implication is that it makes sense to adapt analysis to the needs of some particular users. Targeting analysis toward helping actual partisans interact with each other would increase the chances that research will have some impact on social problem solving, because partisans have incentives to pick up ideas that will help them further their public and private goals by reaching political agreements with others. This would reduce one of the problems now plaguing the policy analysis field: the tendency of government agencies and others to spend heavily on analytical inputs, only to find them not usable.[5]

As obvious as this seems, in fact policy professionals virtually never discuss the thorny issue of how to figure out what their actual or hypothetical clients actually *need*. Policy analysts receive elaborate training in statistics and other aspects of *conducting* research, but very little training in how to decide what is really worth researching given limited time and funds.[6]

Analysis aimed at particular users and adapted to the limited roles that actual participants play in political life necessarily becomes in an important sense "partisan." Although some kinds of partisanship corrupt analysis and lead to inferior policy making, other forms of partisanship are helpful, even necessary to target scarce attention and effort.

What does this imply for the work of policy professionals? Rather than a doomed effort to serve as masterminds, giving advice good for everyone, analysts need to conceptualize their mission along more modest lines. If partisan politics is the mechanism by which public policy must be made, then the modest task of analysis often will be largely to help partisans engage in reasoned persuasion with each other. How could this process of democratic political interaction be strengthened? Many more policy analysts legitimately could embrace the inevitability of partisanship and put themselves explicitly at the service of some set of partisans.

But whom to serve? There is no generic answer to that question, of course. Often, however, the overall competition of ideas can be improved when analysts align themselves with groups that previously have had little analytic help. During licensing hearings for the Three Mile Island nuclear reactor, for example, the intervenor groups opposing a license had to make do with a single professional on their side, whereas the utility company had dozens of economists and other analysts testifying on its behalf. A better balance of partisan-analytic capabilities arguably could have helped bring about an invigorated competition of ideas and better adjustments among the competing ideas and values in civilian nuclear policy.

The competition of ideas about what should be on the political agenda is enhanced when analysts turn attention toward issues they believe deserve

---

[5]Carol H. Weiss, *Using Social Research in Public Policy Making* (Lexington, MA.: D.C. Heath and Co., 1977).

[6]Most clients are themselves not very expert at figuring this out, so simply doing what is requested by a government agency often is a prescription for doing the wrong thing.

higher priority than they are receiving. By way of contrast, the odds are not very high of making a difference when policy professionals align with affluent and well organized causes supporting the status quo and already staffed by numerous experts.

INTELLIGENT TRIAL AND ERROR

One of the tasks that political partisans frequently need help with is coping with uncertainty. To provide this kind of assistance, policy analysts need to take far more seriously the fact that social problem solving ordinarily proceeds through trial-and-error learning based on experience. We need to help partisans figure out how to make the inevitable errors less damaging and how to learn from them more rapidly. Are there institutional arrangements, procedures, and strategies which would help cope better with uncertainty?

Consider three of the main pitfalls in ordinary trial-and-error learning: (1) A policy trial may produce unbearably costly outcomes; (2) policy moves may retain too little flexibility, preventing errors from being corrected readily; and (3) learning about errors may be very slow. More intelligent trial and error would feature strategies for making errors less costly, for building in greater flexibility, and for speeding up the learning process. How might these tasks be approached?

Heading Off Unbearable Errors

How can analysts help political participants cope with potentially unbearable risks? Even in highly uncertain endeavors, one often can partly foresee and protect against some of the worst risks, as homeowners do in obtaining fire insurance as a precaution against catastrophic loss. Likewise, the National Institutes of Health required early biotechnology research to be conducted in special laboratories, sealing in potentially dangerous new organisms. Quite different tactics would be appropriate for other types of problems, but the basic idea is to take some kind of initial precautions rather than merely hoping for the best. The precautions will not prevent errors but will make them less costly.

In 1976–77, when there was no solid, direct evidence that depletion of stratospheric ozone by chlorofluorocarbons was occurring, Congress and the EPA chose to err on the side of caution and acted to ban most aerosol chlorofluorocarbon sprays, even though few other nations did so.[7] In cases like this one, it is fairly obvious what the cautious strategy is. What has to be decided is whether a working majority is willing to pay the costs. In

---

[7]Joseph G. Morone and Edward J. Woodhouse, *Averting Catastrophe: Strategies for Regulating Risky Technologies* (Berkeley, CA: University of California Press, 1986).

other cases, though, analysts have a role to play in posing and answering the question, "If some partisans wanted to be more cautious in protecting against uncertainty in a particular problem area, what policy options would be available to them?"

Flexibility

A second problem with trial-and-error learning is that by the time serious flaws become apparent, a policy may have become quite resistant to change—deeply enmeshed in implementers' careers, in organizational routines, and in the expectations of those comprising a policy network. In framing policy moves, therefore, partisans who actually seek to ameliorate a social problem[8] can improve their odds of success by developing policy options that can be altered fairly readily, should unfavorable experience warrant.

For example, flexibility is higher when a policy's costs are borne gradually, allowing expenditures to be redirected as learning develops. Pressman and Wildavsky characterize this as "payment on performance."[9] In contrast, if payment has to be made in advance—as through large, up-front capital investments—when a program does not work out, investment typically will be irrecoverable, and future options are likely to be unduly limited. NASA's space shuttle illustrates the problem: A launch regime relying on expendable rockets would have been much easier to revamp.[10] Urban job creation programs often have been approached inflexibly—with costly up-front training programs or subsidies to business that could not be recovered when the promised jobs did not actually materialize.[11] If government instead helped businesses to meet their wage bills for each suitably created job, then payment would depend on how many people actually gain employment.

Flexibility also can be enhanced by phasing in a policy during a learning period, a common practice in business; by experimenting in a limited geographical area or for a delimited client base; by simultaneous trials of two or more alternative approaches; by using an existing bureaucracy instead of creating a new, dedicated organization with permanent staff;

---

[8]Obviously, many partisans have goals other than intelligent social problem solving, and they may not want a decision strategy that copes with uncertainty.

[9]Jeffrey L. Pressman and Aaron B. Wildavsky, *Implementation* (Berkeley: University of California Press, 1973), p. 159.

[10]John Logsdon, "The Decision to Develop the Space Shuttle," *Space Policy* 2 (1986):103–19; Ronald D. Brunner and Radford Byerly, Jr., "The Space Station Programme: Defining the Problem," *Space Policy* 6 (1989):131–45.

[11]Pressman and Wildavsky, *Implementation*.

and by many other tactics.[12] Policy analysts potentially can be quite helpful in outlining options for partisans to consider regarding how to enhance flexibility at acceptable cost.[13]

Speeding Up Learning

If political participants and their organizations are to learn more swiftly, feedback from policy trials needs to rapidly reach those with authority to make a change. Feedback often takes too long, allowing accumulation of unfortunate results.[14] Thus, the harmful effects of chlorofluorocarbons were not persuasively documented for nearly half a century after their initial use; it took many years before there was clear evidence that high-rise public housing complexes have a destructive effect on many residents; and a long period had to elapse before researchers could hope to determine whether the Head Start program would produce lasting educational improvements in the children who participated in it.[15]

One response is to rue the misfortune but to consider it an immutable fact of life. Alternatively, partisans can select among policy options partly on the basis of how long it will take to learn whether their effort is on the right track. Since there rarely is enough funding, time and attention, or other resources to tackle all the pressing issues or proposals in a domain, it may sometimes be sensible to favor those problems offering a potential for quick learning.[16] While public policy can hardly match private business in this regard—airlines now alter some fares within a few days if they do not produce the expected changes in travelers' choices—policy making could put far more emphasis on the time lag required for learning.[17]

School reformers, for example, typically have on their agenda a plethora of ills and a bewildering variety of partially contradictory remedies, with no prospect of knowing in advance how well a given proposal will work. Yet

[12]Most standard texts on organizational behavior and public administration do not highlight the need for building in flexibility to facilitate learning from experience, as illustrated by Gregory Moorhead and Ricky W. Griffin, *Organizational Behavior: Managing People and Organizations,* 3rd ed. (Boston: Houghton Mifflin, 1992), and James W. Fesler and Donald F. Kettl, *The Politics of the Administrative Process* (Chatham, NJ: Chatham House Publishers, 1991).

[13]See David Collingridge, *Technology in the Policy Process: The Control of Nuclear Power* (New York: St. Martin's Press, 1983), especially the discussion of flexibility in tactical choice, pp. 191–210.

[14]On the requirements for learning organizations, see Chris Argyris and Donald Schon, *Organizational Learning: A Theory of Action Perspective* (Reading, MA: Addison-Wesley, 1978).

[15]On flexibility and inflexibility, especially in large-scale projects conducted by large organizations, see David Collingridge, *The Management of Scale* (New York: Routledge, 1992).

[16]Of course, a bad policy does not become sensible merely because it has relatively quick feedback. An example of this may be the proliferation of standardized testing in schools where teaching comes to emphasize that which can be readily assessed.

[17]Martha Derthick, *Agency Under Stress: The Social Security Administration in American Government* (Washington, DC: Brookings, 1990).

policy debates do not give priority to those meritorious ideas whose results could be determined fairly quickly. Nor are most other policy domains more attentive to the problem of long-lagged learning, despite the obvious fact that error correction cannot be attempted until feedback emerges.

Some regulatory endeavors do make efforts to speed up learning, however. After numerous bad experiences from chemicals such as PCBs, vinyl chloride, and DDT, the Toxic Substances Control Act of 1976 decreed that all new commercial chemicals would have to be approved by the EPA prior to marketing, partly on the basis of toxicology testing. The Food and Drug Administration long has required elaborate premarket testing and approval of new pharmaceuticals, and medical devices now are subject to screening prior to general release. Such testing is a way of speeding up negative feedback instead of waiting for it to emerge naturally, over a longer period and with greater damage. Ways of achieving this goal obviously would vary across policy areas.[18]

The tasks of learning from experience apply throughout political life. First, since we do not want to step over a cliff while learning, it makes sense to protect against unacceptable risks where feasible. Second, since learning usually takes a while under the best of circumstances, it makes sense to keep policy flexible enough that it can be changed when negative feedback is perceived to warrant. Third, because people and organizations do not automatically learn to do better—indeed, we often have great difficulty learning—it makes sense to prepare deliberately and actively for monitoring, interpretation, and communication of feedback.

One can always devise more precautions, greater flexibility, and increased monitoring, so there is no analytic answer to the question of how far to go in employing these and other strategies. That requires political judgment. But policy analysts in universities, government agencies, interest groups, and think tanks can do much better at framing policy assessments in terms of the requirements for intelligent trial-and-error learning.

REDUCING PROFESSIONAL IMPAIRMENT

Social scientists and policy analysts also need to learn to be more effective investigators. Like all other humans, we have been scarred by the socialization and suppression processes outlined in chapter 10. But professional inquirers have a special obligation to struggle against our impairments by learning to practice skepticism, to provide good evidence and argument, and to become

---

[18]On accelerating feedback, see Morone and Woodhouse, 1986; and Joseph G. Morone and Edward J. Woodhouse, *The Demise of Nuclear Energy?: Lessons for Democratic Control of Technology* (New Haven, CT: Yale University Press, 1989).

more open to challenge.[19] In addition to the biological limitations and socially inflicted impairments we share with other humans, there is an important set of impairments distinctive to professional probers. We need to become aware of these and work to modify them.

Obvious shortcomings conventionally remarked upon include obstructive jargon, weak research design, and a tendency toward excessive statistical quantification.[20] Social analysts are faddish, in part because some are mercenary, willing to do whatever government agencies will fund. Where peer review applies at all, quality control is erratic and inadequate.[21] The list could be extended.

These are nontrivial problems, but we want to focus on a deeper and possibly more important one: Professional policy analysis tends to end up supporting the existing social order and its prevailing distribution of privileges and deprivations. Policy professionals, like all social, physical, and biological scientists, become dependent on elite grants, take employment with elites, seek acceptance by elites, identify with elites.[22]

This comes out, for example, in a tendency for policy-oriented textbooks to assume that the existing system is workable, even benign, rather than challenging its irrationalities and coercive elements.[23] Kelman, for example, takes an explicitly "hopeful view of American government," claiming that "compared with our achievements, our problems and shortcomings seem trivial."[24]

[19]This section is drawn largely from Charles E. Lindblom, *Inquiry and Change: The Troubled Attempt to Understand and Shape Society* (New Haven, CT: Yale University Press, 1990), pp. 192–209.

[20]William Alonso and Paul Starr, eds., *The Politics of Numbers* (New York: Russell Sage Foundation, 1987).

[21]Laurence E. Lynn, Jr., *Knowledge and Politics* (Washington, DC: National Academy of Sciences, 1978); Daryl Chubin and Edward J. Hackett, *Peerless Science: Peer Review and U.S. Science Policy* (Albany, NY: SUNY Press, 1990).

[22]A classic analysis is Karl Mannheim, *Ideology and Utopia* (New York: Harcourt, Brace, 1960); see also Ron Eyerman, Lennart G. Svensson, and Thomas Soderqvist, eds., *Intellectuals, Universities, and the State in Western Modern Societies* (Berkeley: University of California Press, 1987).

[23]Robert A. Heineman, William T. Bluhm, Steven A. Peterson, and Edward N. Kearny, *The World of the Policy Analysts: Rationality, Values, & Politics* (Chatham, NJ: Chatham House Publishers, 1990) call for structural reform of *political institutions*, for example, but do not mention reform of elite privileges. B. Guy Peters, *American Public Policy: Promise and Performance,* 2nd ed. (Chatham, NJ: Chatham House Publishers, 1986), p. 321, calls for the analyst to be "a moral actor as well as a technician," raising questions about the analyst's stance regarding preservation of life, individual autonomy, lying, and fairness, concluding that "it is important for citizens and policymakers to think about policy in ethical terms"—but not actually saying anything that would challenge elite dominance.

[24]Steven Kelman, *Making Public Policy: A Hopeful View of American Government* (New York: Basic Books, 1987), p. 286. Harder to characterize, but worth examining to see how even very thoughtful policy professionals may leave an impression of de facto endorsement of the existing system, are Brian W. Hogwood and Lewis A. Gunn, *Policy Analysis for the Real World* (New York: Oxford University Press, 1984), and Mark E. Rushefsky, *Public Policy in the United States: Toward the Twenty-First Century* (Pacific Grove, CA: Brooks/Cole Publishing Company, 1990).

A British public policy text summarizes studies showing that housing, health care, education, and transport policies belie the belief that massive expansion of government activity in the past half century "benefited primarily the less well off," and that in some cases, in fact, the provision of free education "may actually have promoted greater inequality"; yet the authors do not go on to cast doubt on the overall policy-making process.[25]

The particular failure of policy-oriented textbooks and courses to challenge fundamental features of politics, economics, and culture is in keeping with tendencies in the social sciences as a whole. Thus, a hierarchical bias can be found throughout social thought and throughout the thinking of professional social scientists, who at least implicitly endorse strong authority structures in schools, work organizations, and government. This is despite the fact that there is nowhere to be found a convincing, systematic case showing that people would be worse off, taken all around, from less hierarchical social organization.[26]

Widespread, too, is a tendency to place the burden of proof on professionals who dissent from the mainstream view: critics of the presidential system in the U.S., and critics of the parliamentary system in other nations, for example. Has the dominant set of professional ideas been so carefully processed that it deserves special standing? Are those subscribing to mainstream notions relieved of responsibility for demonstrating the validity of their views? Is there not in fact good reason to believe that consensus tastes among social scientists often represent untested agreements, agreements perhaps symptomatic of professional impairment?

It is not difficult to point to examples of impaired thinking characterizing the two disciplines most closely connected with policy studies, economics and political science. Economists emphasize the usefulness of existing market-oriented systems for resource allocation and capital accumulation, for example, and underemphasize that existing systems divide income unfairly while permitting a small percentage of citizens, known as corporate executives, to direct the productive activities of the mass of citizens, known as employees.

Political scientists portray government in an equally unbalanced way, emphasizing its benign side: "Politics has the function of coordinating the learning processes of the whole society";[27] "political parties are basic institutions for the translation of mass preferences into public policy";[28] people

[25]Martin Burch and Bruce Wood, *Public Policy in Britain,* 2nd ed. (Cambridge, MA: Basil Blackwell, 1989), pp. 217–18, quoting Julian Le Grand, *The Strategy of Equality* (London: Allen & Unwin, 1982), pp. 15, 79.

[26]Larry D. Spence, *Politics of Social Knowledge* (University Park, PA: Pennsylvania State University Press, 1978).

[27]Karl Deutsch, *Politics and Government* (Boston: Houghton Mifflin, 1980), p. 19.

[28]V. O. Key, Jr., *Public Opinion and American Democracy* (New York: Alfred A. Knopf, Inc., 1967), p. 432.

"erect governments to maintain order, further mutual goals, and promote general well being."[29] True enough. But politics also is a mechanism through which elites and others *obstruct* learning; political parties also *mis*represent issues to citizens and try to build electoral machines insulating elected officials from genuine accountability; governments also subjugate, tyrannize, promote some groups' welfare over others, and favor well-organized interest groups over the shared needs of the citizenry as a whole. Failure to note this darker half of politics and economics has the (possibly unintended) effect of muting citizen dissatisfaction, thereby protecting advantaged groups from potential challenges to their advantages.

To improve professional inquirers' contributions to the policy-making process, then, one important task is to reduce professional impairment. This is likely to be a formidable undertaking, since professional impairment is produced by many of the same forces afflicting policy making more generally. If even a minority of those who engage in policy-oriented social analysis become sufficiently concerned, however, they may be able at least to take such steps as promoting a more robust competition of ideas in universities, think tanks, and the rest of the policy field.

CONCLUSION

The quality of public policy depends on a vast network of thought and interaction, in which professional policy analysts play a small role. In any given year or even decade, the actions of governments are not going to be determined in main outline by analysis, reports, books, articles, or pronouncements of those who make a living studying public policy. Time after time the good sense embodied in careful research is ignored, distorted, and otherwise made ineffective. Not atypical was the Reagan administration's policy of eliminating most funding for solar energy technologies just at the time that analysts were coming to agree on their promise.

Over a longer period, though, policy professionals perhaps have a significant role to play in helping hundreds of millions of humans to think more clearly and press more assertively for effective social problem solving. In principle, those who analyze public policy can help to challenge aspects of the policy-making process that obstruct wise policy making, can help to broaden the range of changes under consideration, and can help to deepen political debates about problems, opportunities, and policy options.

To have a better rather than worse chance of fulfilling such hopes, policy professionals need to reconsider what they are trying to do. Rather than aim-

[29]Kenneth M. Dolbeare and Murray J. Edelman, *American Politics,* 3rd ed. (Lexington, MA: D. C. Heath, 1981), p. 7.

ing at remaining neutral, aim for thoughtful and responsible partisanship. Rather than trying to provide correct predictions about an inherently unknowable future, prod political participants to frame policies capable of coping with uncertainty: Give advice about how to take precautions against unacceptable errors, how to build in flexibility, and how to accelerate learning from experience. Rather than accepting the existing political-economic system and policy-making process, challenge where warranted. Rather than aiming analysis solely at political elites, recognize that improved thinking by ordinary people may be humanity's best hope. In short, one of the main tasks of policy professionals should be to help strengthen the competition of ideas.

Chapter *12*

More Democracy?

Why are humans not more effective in actually solving social problems? Why do avowedly democratic governments so often appear unresponsive to many of their citizens? A great many obstacles to intelligent, democratic policy making have appeared chapter by chapter, from which some of the main points now can be distilled.

First, actual and potential participants in policy making do not bring the requisite skills and motivations. Human cognitive limits insure that no one has the capacity to trace all the causes of complex problems or to foresee all the consequences of policy options. Social problems in any case cannot be solved primarily through analysis for all of the reasons discussed in chapter 2. High levels of factual uncertainty make it impossible to fully understand what goes wrong, why, or how to correct it; social life is so complex that deliberate understanding and control over it repeatedly escapes us. Moreover, what some people regard as a solution others see as a problem or failure, and partisans often will differ on what is considered a sufficiently high priority to deserve expenditure of scarce funds. There is no possibility of resolving all such differences by reason alone.

In principle, political interactions among diverse partisans—who mutually adjust to take each other's needs into account in order to win enough support to proceed—can nevertheless evolve policies with significant elements of both intelligence and popular responsiveness. Through trial-and-error learning and other strategic ways of coping with complexity and disagreement, democratic politics offers a sensible way of proceeding with social problem solving (chapter 3).

In practice, however, government turns out to be a clumsy, biased, and only partly controllable instrument for social problem solving. Serious problems persist for years or decades without being acted on, policies often are not monitored carefully enough nor changed quickly in response to negative feedback. One reason for this is that elections are not generally a good method of forming or transmitting thoughtful public judgments about problems or policy options (chapter 4). Elected functionaries are not systematically rewarded for wise or popularly responsive policy making, nor are they systematically punished for poor performance, in part because office holders arrange political institutions to insulate themselves from tight accountability, and in part simply because the complexity of democratic government often makes it impossible to pin blame or determine who to reward (chapter 5).

Although delegation of much policy-making authority to the bureaucracy is essential if a complex government is to work at all, it is impossible to control or even to observe most of the important actions thereby unleashed (chapter 6). These and other defects in governmental institutions are so severe that it is not too much to say that government actually becomes a major part of the problem facing complex societies.

Although interest groups provide essential information and help distill policy issues to manageable proportions, the interest-group system is biased toward serving those with ample funds, organizing abilities, and other resources denied to the majority of citizens (chapter 7). Business in particular has unrivalled access, expertise, funding, and organization that allow it to be a dominant force in political life—slowing down and weakening social problem solving that would be inconvenient for business (chapter 8).

Social and economic inequalities among citizens lead to substantially unequal rates of political participation, to major differences in the effectiveness of their communications with government functionaries, and to great inequalities in the attention paid to their needs and insights (chapter 9). These inequalities continue decade after decade in part because an unequal competition of ideas helps confuse and convince disadvantaged and advantaged alike that great inequality is appropriate, that the fundamentals of the existing system of wealth and privilege ought not be challenged, and that it is foolish, undemocratic, or hopeless to think of revamping political and economic arrangements (chapters 8 through 10).

More generally, the irreducible limitations on human understanding are substantially worsened by social impairments: families, schools, peer groups, work organizations, and other social influences teach us to be less curious, less probing, less skeptical, less demanding than would be desirable for promoting social problem solving (chapter 10).

As a combined result of these and other factors, political participants often set out to pursue policy objectives that make little sense; others, if achieved, actually would be counter productive. Individually and collectively we inevitably make lots of errors, not infrequently make a bad situation worse, and do not sufficiently persist in repeated attempts at correction. Many of us expect impossibly quick results. We often settle for symbolic rather than real solutions. The list could be extended considerably.

Contrary to the impression that some scholarship and teaching about public policy conveys, then, the grave deficiencies in social problem solving are due to deep and enduring features of political-economic processes.[1] Many of the obstacles to intelligent, democratic governance are at least partly inherent in the very nature of political life. Hence, policy making at its best will never live up to the hymns of praise sometimes sung on behalf of democracy.

POTENTIALLY REMEDIABLE DEFICIENCIES

If policy making cannot be excellent on most issues most of the time, does that mean that the world must remain in the same sad shape, that things have to be about as bad as they are? It is impossible to be sure, since no one has the capacity to fully comprehend the causes of complexly interactive social problems. But it appears that many of the gravest deficiencies in public policy are due at least in part to biases and perversities in the policy-making process that potentially could be greatly ameliorated.

It is pretty clear that contemporary democracies actually are only feeble imitations of the aspirations embodied in the word democracy. And the significant undemocratic elements in existing political systems seem to constitute major impediments to more intelligent social problem solving.

The reason why undemocratic processes undermine intelligent policy making, to reiterate, is that the quality of political outcomes is not determined primarily by the quality of elite analysts' ideas, nor even by the insights of the most influential political participants. Policy making is *political,* produced by the interactions of a myriad of participants in a setting of shared power. Hence, what counts most is whether social processes and power relations are set up to promote intelligent inquiry, debate, and mutual adjustment among those with stakes and insights concerning the broad spectrum of social problems and possibilities. When potentially relevant participation is undermined or shut out by systematic biases differentially empowering certain social groups or ideas, less intelligence can be brought influentially to bear.

Naturally, ideas are important in guiding political interactions, and re-

---

[1]This is not to deny that humans need improved understanding of social problems and policy possibilities, including help from policy professionals along the lines discussed in chapter 11. But no more than modest success should be expected of such efforts.

shaped policy ideas emerge from the interactions. But rather than hundreds or even thousands of people, policy making is influenced by millions, hundreds of millions worldwide. At issue is the quality of all their thinking and interaction, regarding all of their problems and potential problems. So we have asked whether social processes help people think clearly and deeply about the problems facing them and their societies—and found that they generally do not. We have asked whether political processes successfully evoke ideas more or less equally from the many diverse people who have a stake in ameliorating social problems—and found that they do not. We have asked whether political institutions give roughly equal weight to each participant's needs and ideas—and found that they do not.

If the political universe is not set up to evoke, receive, negotiate, and act sensibly and fairly on complaints and policy proposals, then potentially good ideas will never have much chance to be developed, debated, and acted upon. Some claims may even be perceived as unintelligible or absurd, especially unconventional ones outside a society's underlying consensus on policy, and especially those voiced by less powerful participants. If many of the ideas needed to ameliorate pressing social problems presently are outside the narrow area of the basic consensus in most nations, then significantly more intelligent policy making will depend on restructuring political institutions and expectations, making cognitive and political room for new ideas.

We believe that existing agreements cripple political institutions and processes, shut many ideas out of active consideration, and stunt substantive problem solving. But that clearly is a partisan judgment. There is no nonpartisan way of determining how serious the world's problems are, and no nonpartisan way of saying what should be done. Those who consider social life to be working fairly well will want to discount to some degree the ideas that follow, as will those who do not believe that political processes can be improved very much.

What would it take to promote diverse, creative debate and to open up new possibilities for policy making, possibilities now foreclosed? No one can say with any certainty. By definition, though, we know it would take far more than conventional analysis by policy professionals: They did not mold the underlying consensus, they alone are not likely to reshape it; and conventional analysis ordinarily takes place *within* the area of consensus. If significantly greater democracy is possible at all in the next century or two, it will have to come about largely via partisan probing and reconsideration, hopefully aided in small but perhaps crucial ways by intellectuals, including policy professionals.[2]

More generally, no one knows for sure how much greater democracy and

---

[2]A thoughtful analysis of a more freely self-examining society is James Fishkin, *The Dialogue of Justice: Toward a Self-Reflective Society* (New Haven, CT: Yale University Press, 1993).

intelligence might be possible; nor can anyone proclaim with certainty what particular changes would be most helpful. Our partisan, imperfect sense of the situation gives priority to reducing three obstructions to fuller, more intelligent democracy: the privileged position of business, inequality, and impaired thought. These elements are tightly interconnected, both in their historical origins and in present practice. We can summarize what has already been said about the impediments and briefly outline steps that might gradually reduce their force.

Acknowledging that our prescriptions are not nearly as well founded as our analysis of the problems, we nevertheless offer prescriptions in hopes that others will react to both their strengths and weaknesses. The intent is to contribute to a very long-term, widespread process of thinking about how feeble democracies can be reshaped into stronger and more intelligent ones.[3]

BUSINESS

As long as what we have called the rival policy-making system of business, along with its many valuable contributions has the legal right and political might to produce disruptive innovations, throw large numbers of people out of work, endanger humans and the environment, and otherwise create significant social problems, there will be sharp constraints on the prospects for intelligent democratic governance. For governments do not do well playing catchup: Inherently a very difficult task, it is made even harder by the privileged position of business and by the accompanying veto powers generously distributed throughout political-economic life.[4] Business activists and their allies are well positioned to slow down or thwart social problem solving.[5]

This is an uncongenial fact, for the state-socialist alternatives clearly have failed in the Soviet Union and elsewhere, with even China and the other surviving communist nations turning increasingly toward market economies. Political-economic thought is nowhere near agreement on how to revise market-oriented economies to preserve valuable features while repairing deficiencies. So one must be somewhat cynical about the realistic prospects and skeptical of schemes that profess to know how it all can be achieved. Must those obstacles constitute a prescription for doing nothing? Perhaps not.

[3]The concept of "strong democracy" is developed by Benjamin Barber in *Strong Democracy: Participatory Politics for a New Age* (Berkeley: University of California Press, 1984).

[4]Catchup also is made harder by other factors, of course, such as deficiencies in the design of governments as mechanisms for social problem solving.

[5]For numerous examples of the political influence of business, together with discussions of the limits of that influence, see David Vogel, *Fluctuating Fortunes: The Political Power of Business in America* (New York: Basic Books, 1989); and Graham Wilson, *Business and Politics: A Comparative Introduction,* 2nd ed. (Chatham, NJ: Chatham House Publishers, 1990).

How far democratic political systems can go in restraining the influence of business in political life is unknowable, except through experience. What can be said is that some nations use more, and more effective, controls than others: more in Israel, fewer in Singapore. And many nations have strategies from which others could learn. For example, Japanese industrial planning and finance ministries like MITI bring corporate executives into close working relations with government and thereby grant substantial authority to business; yet government uses these same working relations to exercise greater influence over business's investment decisions than occurs in the U.S. and other nations.

When business-government relations are looked at from a global perspective, then, a substantial repertoire of control strategies and tactics is available, with reason to believe that the repertoire can be enlarged year by year, as has occurred for the past century and more. Nominations for additional control strategies could focus on limiting the capacity of businesses to turn their natural advantages to political purposes, coupled with shoring up the political resources of other social interests. How might these tasks be approached?

It will be extremely difficult to limit the political use of corporations' access, organization, expertise, and funds without damaging a business's purely economic activities. (Some damage may be worth the gain, of course.) But, in principle, tax deductions could be reduced or eliminated for business expenses incurred for some categories of interactions with government. For example, when the EPA finally issues a new regulation, it routinely is challenged in court by the Chemical Manufacturers Association, another industry association, or by individual companies. All expenses thereby incurred by the business organizations—for attorneys, environmental scientists, secretaries, accountants—presently are tax deductible. If the legal expenses instead had to come entirely out of corporate profits, businesses would be less willing to go to court, and EPA staff members would have to expend a smaller proportion of their scarce time and energy going to court, preparing to go to court, and worrying about the legal challenges that might face an impending regulation.

Alternatively, or in addition, other social interests could be strengthened relative to business. What if a new tax were placed on large businesses and the proceeds used to subsidize consumer-protection activities such as those of Ralph Nader or Consumers Union, antipoverty organizations, environmental groups such as Sierra Club, and good-government organizations like Common Cause? In principle, the tax rate could be increased every few years until it became obvious that the contest between business and other social interests had become more equal. At some level of funding, other interest groups would command sufficient resources to mount more of a real political battle with business.

Another line of attack might come from greater economic democracy, getting corporate executives used to sharing authority with workers in operating their businesses.[6] Thus, in Scandinavia, codetermination laws give workers an influential role in shaping new computer systems and other workplace technologies, thereby empowering workers while raising productivity. American workers, in contrast, have little recourse when management decides to replace skilled workers with robots or close down older factories, as General Motors has been doing for many years. Greater equality between management and labor at work seems to lead, gradually, to more sharing of authority in the political system, and vice versa.

Again, these ideas are merely illustrative, a small sample of those that might deserve consideration. They are politically infeasible at present, and perhaps would be ill advised; after all, one cannot simply wish away the fact that business profitability is required for a market-oriented society to provide the jobs and lifestyles people have come to expect. If the effect of reducing business privileges would be to create economic problems worse than those already inflicted during recessions, many people might prefer to accept the status quo. We believe there are ways of making business profitability compatible with reduced privileges, and that the effects of business privileges on social problem solving are so pernicious that it would be worth the risks to experiment carefully with major alterations to the existing system. But we acknowledge that many thoughtful people may disagree.

REDUCING INEQUALITY

If political equality in policy making requires roughly equal consideration for each person's needs and insights, no contemporary nation comes close to offering equality. Economic, legal, and political-organizational barriers continue to interfere with genuine equality. There has been progress over the past century, however, and further progress is not improbable.

Most nations have substantially removed restrictions on the suffrage, for example, making the right to vote available to previously excluded minority races, women, 18- to 21-year olds, and so forth. Voter registration laws have been eased, poll taxes eliminated, voting booths remain open longer hours to accommodate workers' schedules, and other steps have been taken to make it easier for those supposedly eligible to vote actually to do so. Still, as noted in chapter 4, there is room on this count for considerable improvement, especially in the United States.

A second category of efforts to reduce inequality has involved placing limits on bribery, campaign contributions, speaking fees, and other mechanisms for moving affluent people's money into politicians' hands in exchange

---

[6]Uday Dokras, *Act on Codetermination at Work: An Efficacy Study* (Stockholm: Almqvist & Wiksell, 1990); Jon D. Wisman (ed.), *Worker Empowerment: The Struggle for Workplace Democracy* (New York: Bootstrap Press, 1991).

for favors. Existing laws could be strengthened, as by making penalties more severe. Campaign contributions could be banned altogether, with all election funds coming from the public treasury. And other devices can be imagined. As long as wealthy individuals and institutions need help from government, however, some will find ways to convert their economic resources into political resources.

Other minor tactics for reducing political inequality include periodic redistricting to make sure legislators represent roughly equal numbers of people—a requirement violated by the practice of granting the same number of senators to barely populated Alaska or South Dakota as to heavily populated Texas or California, thereby substantially diluting the voting power of those in the more populous states.

These efforts no doubt have been valuable and important; but such mechanisms reduce only the grossest manifestations of political inequality. What next? In principle, the most effective step would be gradually to move toward equality in the distribution of income and wealth so that no one would have grossly disproportionate economic resources to throw into the political realm.[7] Redistribution of resources obviously would help ameliorate many other social problems (and would create some new problems). But whatever the merits of such a plan, it would be considered absurd in the present climate of opinion. Even minor changes to make taxes more progressive are greeted with massive resistance by those who believe they would lose, and there is little political support for income redistribution even among the poor.[8]

Quite a different tack is recommended by some political scientists who are impressed with the great obstacles posed to governmental action in the United States, where an array of veto powers allow political minorities to slow down or thwart policy making threatening the status quo (see chapters 5 and 7). If presidential vetoes and two houses of Congress thwart social problem solving, this line of argument holds, then constitutional or other changes may be desirable to make it easier for a working majority of elected officials to act together in timely fashion.[9] This could be accomplished by shifting from a presidential to a parliamentary system with little or no separation of authority among branches. Less radically, it could be achieved by eliminating or weakening one house of Congress and revoking the president's veto powers. Very modest progress could be made—too modest to

[7]Separate provisions, such as those discussed above for business, would be necessary to constrain inequalities among institutions.

[8]Jennifer Hochschild, *What's Fair: American Beliefs About Distributive Justice* (Cambridge, MA: Harvard University Press, 1981).

[9]James Sundquist, *Constitutional Reform and Effective Government* (Washington, DC: Brookings, 1987); John E. Chubb and Paul E. Peterson, eds., *Can the Government Govern?* (Washington, DC: Brookings, 1989).

do much good, probably—by requiring presidents and members of their party in Congress to share campaign financing, in the belief that this will draw them together in common cause.[10]

While these proposals have considerable merit, the plain facts are that they would face lethal opposition from entrenched interests and it is just about impossible to pass substantive amendments to the U.S. constitution. An amendment's proponents must jump through extraordinary hoops (two-thirds approval by both houses of Congress, plus thirty-eight state legislatures). Many people, moreover, believe the Constitution to be an infallible work that cannot be improved. So the odds are not very high of reducing political inequality any time soon by constitutional changes aimed at curbing veto powers. But that is no reason for political scientists and policy professionals to shrink from the task of pointing out the relationship between intelligent governance, political equality, and the structural shortcomings of political systems.

REDUCING IMPAIRMENT

A society with high levels of impairment is ill equipped to probe ways of reducing that impairment. So substantial improvements on this obstacle to wise problem solving probably will be just as difficult as reducing inequality or curbing the privileged position of business. If possible at all, impairment will have to be reduced very gradually.

Reformers tend to dream up unlikely ways of drawing citizens into political discussion—such as evenings of group discussions concerning social problems. Perhaps more sensible would be to focus on reducing barriers to inquiry: a less skewed competition of ideas, resulting in less indoctrination of children and adults. While difficult, such curbs on impairing influences would not require anything like a transformation of the human character.

Competition of Ideas

If intelligent, democratic policy making requires mutual adjustment among those concerned with a problem, what is required for a working majority of those people to reach a well-probed, reasoned judgment on how to proceed? Among other helpful contributions to that cause will be having in circulation a diverse set of ideas on the subject in question. Great diversity will help

---

[10]David Mayhew finds that conflict between Republican presidents and Democratic majorities in the House and Senate has not actually made the nation less governable than when the same party controlled both Congress and the presidency. Minor reforms designed to avoid split control therefore probably would achieve little. See David Mayhew, *Divided We Govern: Party Control, Lawmaking, and Investigations, 1946–1990* (New Haven, CT: Yale University Press, 1991).

prevent careless, grossly simplistic, premature agreement on policies that do not offer much prospect of ameliorating the problem.

Perhaps the most substantial change that would need to be made is for millions of people to become concerned about the impairing influences of businesses, families, schools, churches, media, and politics. At present, most of us want to "teach"—or socialize, or indoctrinate—our children and other people into believing as we do about religion, politics, sexual habits, and other aspects of thought and consequent behavior. *Very* low on most people's agendas—no higher than lip service, in fact?—is the notion of actually helping others (or oneself) to become a competent prober. This is true in part because it would require giving up a measure of control, and this would go against our normal use of interpersonal communications as means of extending our control over children, students, coworkers, whomever. If genuinely encouraged to think for themselves, people are unlikely independently always to agree with their parents, teachers, ministers, bosses, or political authorities.[11]

Since communications in every arena of social life are loaded with impairing potential, and we all are used to it, there can be no quick fix. We do not even know how to think very well about what a fix would be.[12] Better inquiry into the matter of how to evolve a significantly less impairing way of life probably must wait until more people become interested in the subject.

One very small step in that direction would focus on reducing the influence of money on effective freedom of speech. On reflection, everyone recognizes that in a "technologically complex society, access to the mass media is a necessary condition for a voice to contribute to the national political debate, (yet) political action committees and corporate contributions serve to distort access to the media."[13] In contrast to the aspiration to provide public schooling and medical care even to the very poor, no comparable expectation or political agitation yet has arisen with regard to political communication by the poor.

Effective political communication ordinarily requires huge sums available only to a small minority of individuals, and even only to a small percentage of organizations. If enough people want to change this, inequalities might be narrowed by making access to communication channels less dependent on money. In principle, for example, it would be possible to allocate a small amount of free television time to every citizen annually, and to allow each to

---

[11]That we are so far away from any widespread awareness of the need to be concerned about impairing influences throughout society is another bit of evidence documenting how serious is the problem of impairment: A relatively unimpaired society would be keenly aware of the few remaining sources of impairment.

[12]See, for example, Jurgen Habermas, *Knowledge and Human Interests* (Boston: Beacon Press, 1971), especially chapters 3 and 9. While insightfully discussing the magnitude of the problems and tracing some of the causes, Habermas and others do not offer clear proposed solutions.

[13]James S. Fishkin, *Democracy and Deliberation: New Directions for Democratic Reform* (New Haven, CT: Yale University Press, 1991), p. 33.

reallocate it to organizations of their choice.[14] Even to get this small reform onto the political agenda seems a gargantuan task; but, over a period of decades, policy debates around such small issues conceivably could kindle interest in attacking the unequal competition of ideas in more fundamental ways.

Another means of broadening the range of ideas under discussion is for social scientists to engage in farther-reaching inquiries. From introductory college courses to sophisticated professional meetings, ideas that really help to challenge the audiences' ways of thinking are few and far between. Yet the opportunities are legion. For example, how might systems of government be designed to have a better chance of catching up with the social problems created via the rival policy-making system centered around corporate executives and consumers? Among other attributes of more effective political systems, government functionaries presumably would need powerful incentives for social problem solving, as well as high competence at it. Contemporary political institutions provide only weak incentives to elected functionaries for actually ameliorating social problems. How monetary, electoral, or other rewards might be more effectively linked with officeholders' success in tackling social problems is a fascinating and important challenge for political science. More importantly, discussions of the problem and proposed remedies also could help enlighten millions of people by challenging them to think harder and better about the current predicament.

Serious reconsideration of business prerogatives, debate about reduction of inequality, and inquiry into the need for reduced impairment is blocked in part by the public's lack of skill at probing either substantive problems or political procedures. Closely connected with lack of skill is lack of motivation or will. Contemporary political science and public policy discussions tend to accept (or omit) the fact that many people, perhaps a majority, are relatively incompetent citizens. It would not be right to blame the victims, of course, and all of us are to some degree victims of impairment. Until the challenge of developing a thoughtful citizenry is put on the agenda of technological societies, however, we cannot rightfully claim to be working toward wiser policy making.

CLOSING THOUGHTS

Impaired probing, political inequality, and the privileged position of business are far from the only reasons governments develop policies that do not succeed, of course. The tasks of public policy making are exceedingly difficult.

---

[14]Even more effective—but even less politically feasible—would be to reduce inequalities of income and wealth, so that funds for political communication are more evenly shared.

Because the world is so complex, human understanding so limited, and organizational life so complicated and problem-ridden, it is reasonable to suppose that public policies often will turn out to disappoint.

But even after absorbing a large measure of realism, it remains true that the policy-making process too often is insufficiently intelligent and insufficiently responsive to ordinary people. Policy outcomes too often are bizarre or monstrous—over one trillion dollars expended just in the 1980s on suicidal nuclear weaponry, medical costs escalating out of control, an energy non-policy allowing depletion of scarce fossil fuels while warming climate and creating acid rain.[15]

We have no easy counsel to offer. The impediments have not been markedly reduced in our lifetimes, and it is difficult to be very optimistic about the foreseeable future. But each of the obstacles to a less-feeble and more intelligent democracy is potentially remediable, at least in part, if enough people become aware of the obstacles and seek changes persistently and competently. Minor modifications such as electoral spending restrictions will not be nearly enough, however. Any society serious about moving toward intelligent democratic governance will have to be willing to debate fundamental features of its economic, political, and social organization. And it will have to acknowledge the inevitability of proceeding via trial and error, reorganizing social life and social thought to better promote strategic learning from experience.

The single most important step in these directions would be to develop a more equal competition of ideas. Such a move would strike simultaneously at the privileged position of business, at inequality, and at impaired capacities for thinking about social problems and policy options. At present, there is inadequate willingness and capacity to take on this challenge, even in universities. But we remain committed to the effort, and hope to be surprised by the next generation.

Name Index

Abelson, Philip H., 21
Aberbach, Joel D., 68, 70
Adamany, David W., 100
Agree, George E., 100
Alonso, William, 135
Anderson, James, 10
Argyris, Chris, 133
Arian, Asher, 40
Arrow, Kenneth, 40
Arterton, F. Christopher, 45
Asmus, Peter, 30

Bachrach, Peter, 11
Barber, Benjamin, 46, 143
Barber, James David, 52
Bardach, Eugene, 57
Barker, Jane, 8
Bauer, R. A., 83
Beck, James M., 58
Beck, Paul Allen, 41
Beer, Samuel H., 54
Beloff, Max, 40
Benda, Peter M., 14
Benedict, Ruth, 120

Bentham, Jeremy, 20
Benveniste, Guy, 59, 70
Bernstein, Robert A., 36
Berry, Jeffrey M., 83
Blais, Andre, 65
Blank, Stephen, 94
Blau, Peter M., 59
Bluhm, William T., 135
Botwinick, Aryeh, 11
Bowles, Samuel, 116
Brady, Henry, 115
Brayman, Harold, 93
Brewer, Garry D., 127
Brokaw, Tom, 118
Brown, Lester R., 27
Brumbaugh, R. Dan, Jr., 49, 82
Brunner, Ronald D., 132
Bryner, Gary, 16, 60, 70, 92
Buchanan, W., 83
Burch, Martin, 136
Burnham, Walter Dean, 59
Burns, James MacGregor, 52
Bush, George H. W., 26, 36, 37, 44, 52–
    53, 91, 95

Butler, Stuart, 15
Byerly, Radford, Jr., 132

Campbell, Angus, 108
Chubb, John E., 78, 146
Chubin, Daryl, 135
Cline, William R., 128
Clinton, Bill, 3, 25, 44, 47, 91
Cloward, Richard A., 108
Cohen, David K., 16, 17
Coleman, James S., 18
Collingridge, David, 21, 30, 62, 128, 133
Converse, Philip E., 108
Corcoran, Paul E., 119
Cowan, Ruth Schwartz, 91

Dahl, Robert A., 4, 41, 46, 48, 96, 105, 120, 145
Delaney, James J., 101
deLeon, Peter, 127
Dempster, Michael A. H., 27
Derthick, Martha, 133
Destler, I. M., 54
Deutsch, Karl, 30, 136
Dexter, L. A., 83
Dickson, David, 62
DiIulio, John J., Jr., 64
Dion, Stephane, 65
Dodd, Lawrence C., 54
Dolbeare, Kenneth M., 137
Dorcas, Uday, 145
Dorgan, Byron, 55
Douglass, Bruce, 19
Downing, Hazel, 8
Drew, Elizabeth, 18
Dryzek, John, 22, 32
Dukakis, Michael, 36, 37
Dunleavy, Patrick, 65
Dye, Thomas R., 34

Edelman, Murray J., 63, 84, 115, 137
Edsall, Thomas Byrne, 100, 101
Ehrenhalt, Alan, 39
Eidlin, Fred, 76, 80
Einstein, Albert, 74
Erikson, Robert S., 36, 37
Etzioni, Amitai, 27
Eulau, H., 83
Eyerman, Ron, 135

Fenno, Richard F., 39
Ferguson, L. C., 83
Fesler, James W., 61, 69, 133

Fiorina, Morris, 58
Firor, John, 128
Fishkin, James S., 46, 142, 148
Flavin, Christopher, 27
Foreman, Christopher H., Jr., 70
Forester, John, 32
Fraser, W. R., 116
Friedrich, Carl J., 59

Gans, Herbert J., 3
Garn, Jake, 82
Gaydos, Joseph M., 101
Gecas, Viktor, 117
Gibbs, Lois, 30
Ginsberg, Benjamin, 119
Gintis, Herbert, 116
Gitlin, Todd, 118
Gonzalez, Henry, 101
Goodin, R., 27
Goodsell, Charles T., 14, 58
Gore, Albert, 101
Grant, Wyn, 95
Greenwood, Ted, 54
Greider, William, 15, 46, 55
Greif, Bill, 101
Greve, Michael S., 77
Grewer, Garry, 127
Griffin, Ricky W., 133
Gruber, Judith, 71
Gunn, Lewis A., 135
Gutman, Herbert G., 116
Guzzardi, Walter, Jr., 101

Habermas, Jurgen, 148
Hackett, Edward J., 135
Hadden, Susan, 97
Hamlett, Patrick W., 150
Hand, Lloyd, 101
Hanushek, Eric, 18
Hardin, Russell, 19
Hartmann, Heinz, 99
Hayes, Michael T., 27, 28
Heineman, Robert A., 135
Hermann, Tamar, 40
Hess, Robert D., 116, 117
Hitler, 23
Hochschild, Jennifer L., 28, 124, 146
Hoffman, P. J., 41
Hogwood, Brian W., 135
Hrebenar, Ronald J., 75
Hummel, Ralph P., 58

Hyman, Herbert, 108
Hyneman, Charles S., 58

Iyengar, Shanto, 118

Jackson, Brooks, 49, 82
Jacobs, Lawrence R., 35
Jasanoff, Sheila, 62
Jennings, Peter, 118
Jewell, Malcolm E., 54
Johnson, Chalmers, 91
Johnson, Lyndon, 108
Jones, Charles O., 14, 41

Kagan, Robert A., 57
Kahneman, Daniel, 115
Kane, Edward J., 82
Kaplan, Sheila, 82
Katznelson, Ira, 115, 116
Kearny, Edward N., 135
Keating, Charles, 58, 111
Keating Five, 58, 111
Keefe, William J., 41
Keeter, Scott, 42
Kelman, Steven, 135
Kettl, Donald F., 61, 69, 133
Key, V. O., Jr., 79, 136
Kinder, Donald R., 118
Kingdon, John W., 10, 22
Kissinger, Henry A., 16, 74
Kohl, Helmut, 102
Kohlmeier, Louise A., 94
Kohn, Melvin L., 117
Konda, Thomas Milan, 119
Kraft, Michael, 71, 77
Krepinevich, Andrew F., Jr., 64

Lamb, Curt, 108
Lampton, David M., 61
Landau, Martin, 70
Lang, Gladys Engel, 42
Lang, Kurt, 42
LaPalombara, Joseph, 80
Le Grand, Julian, 136
Levine, Arthur L., 50
Levine, Charles H., 14
Lieberman, Joseph I., 27
Lieberthal, Kenneth G., 61
Lindblom, Charles E., 7, 16, 17, 22, 25, 27, 28, 66, 90, 114, 123, 135
Lipsky, Michael, 59, 63
Logsdon, John, 132
Long, Samuel, 35

Lowi, Theodore J., 41, 50, 70
Lustick, Ian, 28
Luttbeg, Norman R., 36
Lynn, Laurence E., Jr., 135

MacKenzie, Donald, 8
Mannheim, Karl, 135
Mansbridge, Jane J., 35
Maria, Berad, 95
Marks, Marc L., 101
Marx, Karl, 121
Mashaw, Jerry L., 57
Mason, Edward, 59
Maxwell, Nan L., 97
Mayhew, David R., 54, 55, 56, 63, 147
Maynes, Mary Jo, 115
Mazmanian, Daniel A., 77
McCaffrey, David P., 64
McClosky, Herbert, 41
McConnell, Grant, 94
McCubbins, Mathew D., 69
McFarland, Andrew S., 87
Mele, Don A., 99
Meyer, Marshall W., 59
Miller, Warren E., 108
Miyazawa, Kiichi, 100
Moorhead, Gregory, 133
Morone, James A., 88
Morone, Joseph G., 19, 30, 62, 131, 134

Nader, Ralph, 144
Nelkin, Dorothy, 51
Niemi, Richard G., 42, 106, 107
Nisbet, Richard E., 115

O'Hagan, Anne, 78
O'Hara, Rosemary, 41
Oppenheimer, Bruce I., 54
Orren, Gary R., 119

Page, Benjamin I., 97
Parker, Glenn R., 42
Pastore, John O., 128
Patterson, Samuel C., 54
Peele, Gillian, 40
Perot, H. Ross, 43, 44, 48, 74, 85, 95, 110
Perrow, Charles, 19
Perrucci, Carolyn C., 91
Persell, Caroline Hodges, 116
Peters, B. Guy, 59, 135

Peterson, Paul E., 78, 146
Peterson, Steven A., 135
Phillips, Kevin, 46
Piasecki, Bruce, 30
Pickle, Jake, 101
Piven, Frances Fox, 108
Plato, 23
Pollak, Michael, 51
Polsby, Nelson W., 11, 22
Pool, I. de Sola, 83
Powell, G. Bingham Powell, Jr.,
    106
Pressman, Jeffrey L., 132
Putnam, Robert D., 70

Qualter, Terence H., 118
Quayle, Dan, 93

Rabkin, Jeremy, 71
Rae, Douglas, 40
Rather, Dan, 118
Reagan, Ronald, 102
Reeve, Colin, 21, 128
Reichley, A. James, 73
Richman, Alvin, 37
Rivlin, Alice M., 17
Rizzi, Bruno, 59
Rockman, Bert A., 70
Rogow, A. A., 98
Rose, Richard, 106
Rosenbaum, James, 116
Rosenbaum, Walter A., 60, 71
Rosenberg, Morris, 117
Rosenstone, Steven J., 106, 107
Ross, Lee, 115
Rourke, Francis E., 59
Rule, Wilma, 78
Rushefsky, Mark E., 62, 135

Sabato, Larry, 73, 81
Safran, William, 76, 78, 80
Sanera, Michael, 15
Schattschneider, E. E., 87
Schlozman, Kay Lehman, 83, 102,
    110
Schneider, Stephen J., 128
Schon, Donald, 133
Schonfield, William, 116
Schulman, Paul R., 27
Schumpeter, Joseph, 34
Schwartz, Nancy L., 76
Schwartz, Thomas, 69
Scott, Ruth K., 75

Shapiro, Robert Y., 35
Shimahara, Nubuo, 115
Shoemaker, Pamela J., 118
Simon, Brian, 116
Simon, Herbert A., 5
Slaton, Christa Daryl, 45
Slovic, Paul, 115
Smith, Adam, 92, 115
Smith, Eric, 42
Smith, Fred L., 77
Smith, James A., 15
Smith, John J., 128
Sniderman, Paul, 115
Sobel, Richard, 35, 37
Soderqvist, Thomas, 135
Sorauf, Frank J., 110
Spence, Larry D., 120, 136
St. Germain, Fernand, 81–82
Starling, Grover, 28
Starr, Paul, 135
Steed, Tom, 101
Steinbruner, John D., 30
Steiner, Gilbert Y., 35
Stokes, Donald E., 108
Stokey, Edith, 127
Stone, Deborah A., 10, 24
Stout, Russell, Jr., 70
Sullivan, Lawrence, 58
Sundquist, James, 78, 146
Sunstein, Cass R., 86
Svensson, Lennart G., 135

Talmud, Ilan, 40
Taylor, Lori, 18
Tedin, Kent L., 36
Thatcher, Margaret, 53, 102
Tierney, John T., 83, 102, 110
Torney, Judith V., 116, 117
Trump, Donald, 74
Turner, Ralph H., 117
Tversky, Amos, 115
Tyack, David B., 116

van Crevold, Martin, 64
Verba, Sidney, 119, 122
Vig, Norman, 71, 77
Vogel, David, 92, 97, 102, 122,
    143

Wahlke, John C., 51, 83
Wajcman, Judy, 8
Waldner, I., 27
Weinberg, Martha W., 59

Weinrod, Bruce, 15
Weir, Margaret, 115, 116
Weisberg, Herbert F., 42, 106, 107
Weiss, Andrew, 32
Weiss, Carol H., 130
White, Lawrence J., 11
Wildavsky, Aaron B., 21, 27, 115,
    132
Wilson, Graham K., 92, 94, 102, 143
Wilson, James Q., 58, 64, 71, 72, 100,
    108
Wisman, Jon D., 145
Wolfinger, Raymond E., 106, 107

Wood, Bruce, 136
Woodhouse, Edward J., 16, 19, 30, 32,
    62, 131, 134
Wright, Charles, 108

Yates, Douglas, 63, 66, 86
Yin, Robert K., 63
Young, Iris Marion, 86

Zeckhauser, Richard, 127
Zeigler, L. Harmon, 34
Zimmerman, Joseph F., 78
Zysman, John, 92

Subject Index

Page numbers followed by t or n indicate tables or footnotes, respectively.

Administrative discretion, 61
Administrators, 60, 61, 62
Advertising, institutional, 99
AFL-CIO, 80, 85
Agenda setting, 11, 21–22, 76
Agreement
  in lieu of complete understanding, 24–26
  search for, 25–26
Air Force Association, 74
Alternative policies, 123
American Bar Association committees, 84
American Business Conference, 99
American Enterprise Institute, 15
American Jewish Congress, 74
American League to Abolish Capital Punishment, 87
American Medical Association (AMA), 74, 77
American Postal Workers Union, 74
Analysis, 32
  adapting, to politics, 127–131
  for conflict resolution, 128–130

fallibility of, 16–19
with focus mostly on ills to be remedied, 28–29
with focus on few policy options, 28
fragmentation among partisans, 30–31
improving, 127
incremental, 27–29, 32
for intelligent trial and error, 131–134
limits on, 15–22
making the most of, 126–138
partisan, 128–131
versus power, 6–7
problem formulation and, 21–22
public interest criterion, 19–20
role of
  in budgeting, 129
  in persuasion, 129
strategic, 26–30, 32
targeting, 130
time and cost of, 20–21
by trial and error, 29–30, 32
ubiquity of, 13–15
who can be trusted to do, 6n

Antipathy, 115
Antipoverty programs, 108
Appointed functionaries, 45, 46
Appointed officials, 4. *See also* Appointed functionaries
Assistant Secretary of Energy, 67
Audubon Society, 69
Australia
  Commission on the Future, 14
  unions in, 95
Austria, employers' organizations in, 95
Authority, fragmentation of, 48

Brazil, 62
Britain
  Conservative Party, 53
  Labour Party, 80
  National Economic Development
    Council, 15
  parliamentary politics, 50
  prime minister and cabinet, 51
  single-member districts in, 39
  Thatcher era, 80
  Thatcher government, 92
Brookings Institution, 15
Budget(s)
  deficits, 18
  setting, analysis in, 129
  unbalanced, 18
Bureaucracy, 57, 58, 140
  democratic supervision of, 68–71
    versus intelligent supervision, 70–71
Bureaucratic intelligence, 62–65
  limitations on, 63–65
Bureaucratic policy making, 57–72
Bureaucrats, 58, 59–61
  behavior of, 71, 72
Bush administration, 52
  and recession of 1990–92, 54
  refusal to sign Rio biodiversity treaty,
    62
Business, 90–103, 140, 143–145
  advantages of, 124
    in electoral politics, 99–101
  control of
    government, 102, 103
    range and kinds of, 93–96
    strategies for, 144–145
  cycle of, 92
  electoral activity of, 103
  financial support of, from government, 102

incentives and sanctions for, 123
influence on policy, 101–102
  forms of, 96–101
needs of, 98
neglect of, 93
political strength of, 102
privileges, 90–93, 95–96
  categories of, 93–94
roles of
  leadership, 91
  policy-making, 7–9
  in politics, 102–103
subsidies, 102
tax concessions, 102
tax deductions, 144
Business and Defense Services Administration (BDSA), 94
Business executives, 8–9, 91–93
  earnings of, 97–98
  electoral controls, 96–97
  functions of, 7
  persuasion of citizens by, 97–99
  tax favors, 97
Business funds, 99–100
  political use of, 100, 100n
Business interest organizations, 102
Business Roundtable, 101

Cabinet ministers, 45
Campaign funds, 80–82
  contributions to, 146
Canada, 62
  coordination in, 52
Carter Administration, 66
Catchup, 143, 143n
Checks and balances, 48
Chemical Manufacturers Association,
  144
Childrearing, power-oriented, 117
China, 143
Chlorofluorocarbons, 90–91, 131, 133
Church League of America, 74
Citizens
  inequality among, 140. *See also* Political inequality
  influence on policy, 35, 35n
  persuasion of, by business, 97–99
  wants of, clarifying and articulating,
    75–76
Citizens Clearinghouse for Hazardous
  Waste, 30n
Civics education, 116

Civil servants, 45. *See also* Appointed
functionaries
role of, 59, 61, 61n
Clean Air Act, 93
Coalition building, 78–79
Codetermination laws, 144–145
Cognitive limits and impairments, 5–6
Coleman report, 17–18
Common Cause, 85
Common interests, subordination of, to
segmental interests, 86–87
Communication(s)
effective, 148–149
unilateral, from elite to mass, 118–119
Competition of ideas, 7, 122, 130–131,
147–149
strengthening, 138, 150
Compliance, voluntary, 92
Conflict resolution
analysis for, 128–130
methods of, 128–129
Congress, 38, 39, 47, 51, 54, 57, 60, 131.
See also House of Representatives; Senate
acts of, 61
committees, 49–50, 74. *See also specific committee*
environmental subcommittees, 69
internal organization of, 56
low turnover in, 81
members of, 74
micromanagement of, 70
newsletters, 54
oversight, 68n, 68–69
party control of, 146–147, 147n
Congressional Budget Office, 14
Congressional Research Service, 14
Consensus, 120
Constitution, 35, 147
Consumer influence, 8
Coordination, 49–53, 65–68
centralized, versus mutual adjustment,
66–68
sufficient, 68
Criminal justice policy, goals of, 63–64

Decision making, intelligent, implications of elected functionaries for,
55–56
Deference, 111
Deficiencies, potentially remediable,
141–143
Deficits, 18

Democracy, 2, 32, 54
complications of, 47–49
contemporary, 141
and inequality, 104–106
intelligence of
inequality and, 112
potential, 23–32
need for more, 139–150
obstacles to, 141
versus private enterprise, 98–99
strong, 143, 143n
systems of, 52
Democratic Party, 40, 41, 50
Democratic policy making, complications of, 47–49
Democratic politics, 7
Denmark, voter turnout in, 107
Department of Agriculture, 14
food stamp program, 58
Department of Commerce, 94
Department of Energy (DOE), 66, 67
radioactive waste disposal program,
58
Department of Labor, 65
Division of labor, 65–66
Drexel Burnham Lambert, 82

Economic growth, 91
Economics, impaired thinking in, 136
Economic system, 121
Education, 115–120
courses, failures of, 136
creative, 71
Educational policy, 66
Egalitarians, 105
Elected functionaries, 45–56, 60, 68, 71,
140
implications for popular control and
for intelligent decision making,
55–56
mechanisms for holding accountable,
53
self-selected roles of, 53–55
Elected officials, 4. *See also* Elected
functionaries
Elections, 140. *See also* Voting
effects of interest groups on, 80
goals served by, 43
U.S., 1990, 39
Electoral College, 48
Electoral politics
advantages of business in, 99–101
European-style, 53

Elite
  advantage of, impairment and, 120–124
  unilateral communications from, to mass, 118–119
Employers' organizations, 95
Endangered Species Act, 53
Energy conservation, 27, 86
Energy policy, French, 51
Enforcement of policies, 60
Environmental Defense Fund (EDF), 74, 77
Environmental laws, enforcement of, 60
Environmental protection, 86
  programs, 41
Environmental Protection Agency (EPA), 30, 57, 62, 69, 77, 128, 131, 134, 144
Equality. *See also* Inequality
  alternatives, 104–105
  political
    meaning of, 105
    norm of, 104, 105–106
Equal Rights Amendment, 35
Errors, heading off, 131–132
Ethyl Corporation, 128
Executive leadership, 51–53
Executive Order 12291, 14

Fair housing laws, 29
Farm Bureau Federation, 74
Farm policy, 86
Favors, 111
Federal Communications Commission (FCC), 60, 72, 94
Federal Election Commission, 81
Federal Reserve, 68
Federal Reserve Board, 62
Federal Trade Commission, 94
Feedback, 133n
Fergus Falls Chamber of Commerce, 74
Fire-alarm method, 69
Flexibility, 132–133
Florida Dairy Products Association, 74
Food and Drug Administration, 57, 134
Food stamp program, 58
Foreign policy, 54
Foreign-trade policy making, 83
Fragmentation, 66
  of analysis, among partisans, 30–31
  of authority, 48
France
  Commissariat du Plan, 15

energy policy of, 51
Garn Institute, 82
National Assembly, 48
secondary education in, 116
voting in, 38
Free speech, 119
  influence of money on, reducing, 148
  right of, 75
Functionary, 4
  access to, 101
  appointed, 45, 46
  elected. *See* Elected functionaries
Funding, 60, 109–111
  business, 99–100
  campaign, 80–82

General Accounting Office (GAO), 14, 68
  reports on energy policy, 16
General Electric, 91, 94
General Motors, 96, 145
Germany, 43. *See also* West Germany
  Bundesrat, 70
  Christian Democratic Union (CDU), 40
  Deutches Bundesbank, 62
  labor in, 80
  Ministry of Trade, 92
  Parliament, 48, 70
  political parties and voting in, 40
  Social Democratic Party (SDP), 40
  Wissenschafts-zentrum, 14
Government, monitoring, 77
Government officials. *See* Functionary; public official(s)
Government policy making, 7
Grace Commission, 14
Green Party, 39, 43

Hazardous waste dumps, cleanup of, 30, 30n
Head Start program, 133
Heritage Foundation, 15
Honda, 96
Honoraria, 82
House Banking, Finance and Urban Affairs Committee, 81
House of Representatives, 39, 49
House Science, Space and Technology Committee, 50

Housing policy, 29
  targets for, 28

Ideas. *See* Competition of ideas
Impairment. *See also* Inquiry, impaired
  and elite advantage, 120–124
  of policy professionals, 134–137
  reducing, 134–137, 147–149, 148n
  sources of, 115–120, 140
Implementation, 11
Income redistribution, 121, 146, 146n
Incremental analysis, 27–28
Incrementalism, 32
Indoctrination, 121–124
Inducements, 92
Industrial regulations, 86
Inequality
  among citizens, 140
  attacks on, 122
  causes of, 107–109
  democracy and, 104–106
  in information, 107
  and intelligent policy making, 111–113
  issues of, 9
  political, 9–10, 85–86, 104–113
  reducing, 145–147, 149n
  socioeconomic, 9–10
Information
  availability of, 16
  demand for, 6–7
  inequality in, 107
  too much and too little, 18–19
Information-acquiring activities, during
      recent American election cam-
      paigns, percentages engaging in,
      107
Informed persuasion, effectiveness of,
      83
Inquiry
  impaired, 114–124. *See also* Impairment
    results of, 120
    skills of, 124
Institutional advertising, 99
Intelligence
  bureaucratic, 62–65
  criteria for, 25
  of democracy, potential, 23–32
  inequality and, 111–113
Interactive policy making, 24, 26
Interest groups, 73–88, 140
  activity of
    clarifying and articulating what cit-
      izens want, 75–76
    coalition building, 78–79

forming feasible agenda, 76
    indispensability of, 75–79
    interactive problem solving, 77–78
    monitoring governance, 77
    persuasion, 82–84
    subordination of common to seg-
      mental interests, 86–87
  effects of
    on elections, 80
    sources of, 79–84
  leaders of, 84
  political inequality of, 85–86
  surveillance function of, 77
  troublesome aspects of, 84–88
Interstate Commerce Commission, 60
Interstate commerce law, 60
Iran-Contra affair, 41, 54
Israel, 144
  Knesset, 45
  Labor Party, 39–40
Issues
  primary, 123
  secondary, 122–123

Japan, 62
  bureaucracies, 58
  coordination in, 52
  Diet, 45
  government agencies, 92
  government of, 91
  Japanese Federation of Economic Or-
      ganizations (*Keidanren*), 94–95
  labor interests, 80
  Liberal Democratic Party (LDP), 100
  Lockheed scandal, 100
  Ministry of International Trade and
      Industry (MITI), 15, 91n, 144
  Recruit scandal, 100
  Socialist Party, 80
  trade associations, 94
  voting in, 38
Jobs, 91
  urban creation programs, 132
Joint Chiefs of Staff, 74
Junk bond salespeople, 121

Labeling, 97
Labor
  division of, 65–66
  relations with, 86
  unions, 110
Latex Foam Rubber Council, 74
Leadership, executive, 51–53

Learning, speeding up, 133–134
Legislative party. *See* Political party
Legislature, organization and coordination in, 49–50
Libertarian rules, 47–48
Liberty, complications of, 47–49
Loan guarantees, to business, 102
Lobbying, 74–75
Lobbyists, 83, 83n. *See also* Interest groups
Local problems, 5
Lockheed, 100
Love Canal, 30n

Majority rule, 48
Market-oriented society, 7
    effect on government actions that restrain business, 103
Market socialism, 16
Market systems, 112–113
Mass(es), unilateral communications from elite to, 118–119
Media, 117–118
Military, 64–65
Misrepresentation, 97
Mobil Oil, 99
Money, influence on effective freedom of speech, reducing, 148
Moral issues, 41
Mothers Against Drunk Driving (MADD), 86–87
Mutual adjustment, versus centralized coordination, 66–68

NASA
    Challenger space shuttle disaster, 50
    Hubble Space Telescope fiasco, 50
    space shuttle, 132
National Association for the Advancement of Colored People (NAACP), 83–84
National Association of Manufacturers, 85
National defense, 86
National Institutes of Health, 131
National Rifle Association (NRA), 74
National Welfare Rights Organization, 108
Natural Resources Defense Council (NRDC), 77
Netherlands, 43
Nissan, 96
Nixon Administration, 54

Nixon White House, 94
Non-elites, 123–124
Norway, 85
    voter turnout in, 107
Nuclear regulatory agencies, 62

Obfuscation, 121–124
Occupational Safety and Health Act, 65
Occupational Safety and Health Administration (OSHA), 64, 71
Office of Education, 66
Office of Management and Budget (OMB), 14, 129
Office of Technology Assessment, 14
    studies undertaken by, 21
Official(s). *See* Public official(s)
Organization(s)
    availability of, 100–101
Organizing, 49–53
    for political participation, 109–111
Oversight, congressional, 68n, 68–69

Paper Bag Institute, 74
Parliamentary systems, 51, 60, 69
Partisan analysis, 128
    fragmentation of, 30–31
Partisanship, 24–25, 26, 31
    goals of, 132, 132n, 138
    and oversight, 69
    thoughtful, 129–131
    ways to think about making and responding to policy proposals, 25–26
Payment on performance, 132
Payroll, 91
Peer groups, 117
Performance, payment on, 132
Persuasion, 82–84
    informed, effectiveness of, 83
    nonrational and irrational, 128
    reasoned, 129
Planning, 14–15
Planning and zoning commissions, 15
Poland, general strike, 1989, 95
Policy
    classic choice of options, 54
    enforcement of, 60
    evaluation of, 11

Voting (*cont.*)
  imprecision of, 34–44
  mechanisms of, 39–40
  one vote versus many policies obstacle,
    38
  single dimension of, 38
  unequal participation in, 106–107

Washington, D.C., 73
Wealth
  advantages of, 124
  influence of, 110–111

redistribution of, 121, 146, 146n
West Germany. *See also* Germany
  Christian Democratic Union (CDU),
    80n
  Confederation of German Trade
    Unions (DGB), 76, 80n
  Social Democratic Party (SDP), 80,
    80n
White House Council on Competitive-
    ness, 93
Wissenschafts-zentrum, 14
W.R. Grace Co, 99–100